Singleness Redefined

Singleness Redefined

Living Life to the Fullest

Carolyn Leutwiler

P U B L I S H I N G
P.O. BOX 817 • PHILLIPSBURG • NEW JERSEY 08865-0817

Printed in the United States of America

Library of Congress Control Number: 2008929114

ISBN: 978-1-59638-111-7

This book is dedicated to all single women in Christ—
those I have yet to meet and ones I love—
specifically my dear New York City and
Charlotte friends. You know who you are!

And to my nieces, Anna and Lizzie. I love you dearly.

May you all be women of great faith
who live fully for the Lord!

"I have come that they may have life,
and have it to the full" (John 10:10).

Contents

Acknowledgments

SO MANY individuals contributed in different ways to bring this book to fruition. Virginia Spykerman was there at the very beginning when the idea was birthed. Thank you for collaborating on the outline and for walking with me during a huge life transition. Angel Cross has epitomized enthusiasm and enduring friendship, especially at key moments. I am grateful for your encouragement. Debbie Perkins believed this book could be of service to others and prodded me to seek publication; thank you. When needed, Webb Younce graciously offered his expertise; I could not have done it without you. Joel Hathaway introduced me to Dr. Robert Peterson, who immediately started the publishing ball rolling. I am immensely grateful for your assistance and ongoing enthusiasm. Thank you to Marvin Padgett and all the staff at P&R Publishing for giving this book the opportunity to be shared—specifically to Eric Anest for managing the editing process and Kathryn McIntier for responsiveness in the marketing arena.

Pauline Kwong Bridgeman, my lifelong friend, you have always "believed in me" when I doubted. Thank you.

Oh, my dear parents, I am grateful beyond words for your undying love for and support of me. Thank you for struggling with me through the difficult seasons and helping encourage this book to completion. You and your endless prayers and faith have been a sure foundation for me. Thank you, Kathy Jacobs, my sister and the true writer of our family, for your wisdom, love, and support through the years. How blessed I am with my wonderful family.

And finally and foremost, I cannot praise enough my Lord and Savior, who is love everlasting and faithful, even when I am faithless. To him be all glory!

Prologue

SITTING ALONE on a park bench, one finds the panorama for observation and imagination to be endless: sunlight streams through the trees; screams of glee waft from the nearby playground; an elderly lady sits quietly absorbed in thought; a family meanders by, enjoying the warmth of the promising spring day; two lovers stroll hand in hand, exchanging smiles and light conversation. For a moment, place yourself on that park bench surrounded by these sights and these characters, involved in a unique story. What is your response? Contentment? Pleasure? Hope? Unfortunately, many single women tend to drift toward feelings of loneliness or bitterness.

Even if you have not experienced these or similar emotions but you are single, you are among a multitude of lovely, unwed women ranging from twenty-somethings to centenarians. The word *single*, whether referring to a man or a woman, immediately conjures up countless impressions, attitudes, and feelings, even though the definition is simply "one only."[1] This six-letter word has become so complex. The topic of singleness is made up of many layers: countless philosophies, arguments, and attitudes. What do you conclude about singleness when

1. *The Random House Dictionary* (New York: Random House, 1980), 818.

confronted with a (perhaps rare) moment of silence or a cutting rejection from a friend, coworker, or family member? Feelings of isolation might well up, or maybe you try to avoid considering the issue altogether.

For the first several years out of college, I had few thoughts about singleness, simply enjoying the time and seeking adventures before I would undoubtedly be married (in the next several years, of course!). But as the years piled up and one random job after another was added to my résumé and I acquired numerous addresses in several states, a mild depression set in regarding the realities of daily life and a murky future. I felt rudderless and lethargic about my life. I often tried to fill my time with constant activity, people, and noise so that I did not have to confront the feelings and emotions. In truth, I inwardly took pride in all the activities I was juggling. Through all this, however, I sensed that such busyness was not the Lord's intent for my life. So I began searching Scriptures and praying about how I should then live in this present stage of life. I wanted to think rightly about singleness.

Additionally, sharing in the joys and sorrows, fun and frustrations of life with my single girlfriends gave me an intense desire to encourage all of us toward full and abundant life now—where God currently has us. Thus the ideas for this book were birthed.

If you have questions about singleness, desire to grow more abundantly during this life stage, or feel discouraged and too tired to continue on, I hope and pray that some of the words in this book will shed a new light on the significance and joy that we single women can have. I have written these words from my heart—to encourage my dear sisters with whom I have cried and laughed, but also to encourage those of you whom I have not had the opportunity to meet.

1 Tale or Truth?

● ● ● ● ● ● ● ● ● ● ● ● ● ● ●

Once Upon a Time

"Oh, heavens!" she cried. "Where am I?"

The prince answered joyfully, "You are with me," and he told her what had happened, saying, "I love you more dearly than anything else in the world. Come with me to my father's castle, and be my wife."[1]

This fairy tale of Snow White is emblazoned on our hearts from the time of childhood. Many little girls dream of being rescued and swept off their feet by a handsome prince to live happily ever after. We may not have our prince's exact face defined, but we certainly have many of his attributes in mind: dashing, strong, humorous, reliable, and steadfast. Although the idea that a fairy tale could have a profound impact may seem silly and sentimental, I have often pondered the actual effect on little impressionable minds and hearts. Could it be that we really do carry these dreams with us into adulthood (and maybe into marriage for those of us who will be married) much more than we realize?

1. *Classic Fairy Tales* (Seymour, CT: Greenwich Workshop Press, 2003), 60.

Personally, I assumed that I would finish high school, attend college, marry, and have two children—all by age 27! Now that I am beyond that age, I have realized that the Lord's thoughts are not my thoughts, neither are his ways my ways—biblical truth from our Father's mouth in Isaiah 55:8. How often has a scriptural truth such as this cut right to the heart? If we were honest, I'm sure that each of us could admit times of bitterness at hearing these words. Maybe you have been stung with the unanswered reality of singleness—possibly for years. You may ask, "How can marriage *not* be in God's plan for me now?" We can become overwhelmed with disappointment, frustration, and a myriad of other emotions that can eat away at the fibers of our being.

Why can it be so difficult at times to accept and even enjoy life as a single woman?

"Sex, Lies, and Videotape"[2]

We often believe in lies. Deceptions and distorted images discreetly enter our minds, ears, eyes, and hearts and can cause us to struggle in various ways. I truly believe that many of our frustrations stem from a skewed view of reality. Scripture says that the father of lies, Satan, "masquerades as an angel of light" (2 Cor. 11:14). He makes so much that is counterfeit look bright and beautiful. In C. S. Lewis's *The Chronicles of Narnia*, it seems to be no coincidence that the evil power is depicted as a beautiful white witch, not a decrepit old hag. If we were to see the current world, events, and people through spiritual lenses, it would be curious to observe how much is actually deformed.

2. Title borrowed from *Sex, Lies, and Videotape*, directed by Steven Soderbergh (Miramax Films and Showtime Networks, 1989).

The following pages highlight several consistent themes as well as responses to attacks that strike at us as single women.

Un-Reality TV

Reality TV is the rage these days, with countless programs from which to choose. But the whole concept of "reality" TV continues to baffle my mind; it is so absolutely *un*realistic! On the relationship/dating shows, the people are thrown together, often in the most far-fetched circumstances. The situations are handpicked, and many of the details are filtered and perfected. In addition, we track the participants' lives for only a brief time; the future is not seen. How many of these people will end up with happy, healthy relationships once the reward money runs out? And yet, many of us are drawn into these programs. Our minds *will* be affected in some way or another. This is the reality of TV.

Also from the entertainment industry, we are bombarded with images of people who find the "love of their life" in the most uncanny situations. Television and movies paint fascinating and alluring portraits of relationships. Most of them end happily ever after—just as in the fairy tales. Boy meets girl; they face insurmountable obstacles, which they overcome victoriously; and they end rapturously in love—idyllic but often missing the full commitment into marriage. Furthermore, in real life, we know that in their offscreen lives, quite a few actors are in highly unstable relationships, unable to re-create their movie romance in their daily existence. And yet, we scour the magazines for news on the latest Hollywood couple or check the Web sites for the most recent love interest of our favorite movie star. Do we somehow think we can live vicariously through these tabloid romances? Even though the temptation

15

to jump into the craze is great, when I step back from all the fanfare, I truly can see no lasting benefit.

The Island of Misfits[3]

Most of us have experienced that awkward moment in church when someone wants to set us up with the boy next door—or, boy in the next pew. Or perhaps you have endured the woes of a lame singles' event. These uncomfortable realities might tempt you to quit going to church altogether.

Our churches are not always nurturing places for single women. Instead of being accepted as viable participants in the visible church, we are sometimes unwittingly excluded from its vibrant dynamics. Some of our churches see singles as having a "missing part" without a husband or as being capable of operating at only half-steam. This mistaken idea takes me back to my childhood days with Rudolph (yes, the Reindeer) and his forgotten friends. Because of their missing limbs or parts that didn't operate quite as expected, they were sent to the land of misfit toys. After a little love and attention from Santa, however, they ended up having a vital role to play. It seems that they were mis*judged*, not misfit. We must pray that the church body would see us as God does: equipped at this time in our lives just as God wishes us to be.

I'm afraid that singles themselves don't often help to change the perception. By our negative attitudes, lethargy, and reluctance to become involved in the church or the community, we build walls around ourselves. Instead, why not shift your attitude and get involved positively? We will explore in a later chapter ways to give of your talents to the church. Many of us have more time available to serve than our married friends do. Our schedules are freer. Seize this unique circumstance to be

3. Title borrowed from *Rudolph the Red-Nosed Reindeer*.

used by God, to make a commitment to his church. Do not present the church with an opportunity to form a misjudged opinion of the single!

Sex and the City

Sex is everywhere: on TV, in movies, on billboards, in books, in conversation, and practically everywhere else. In your personal life, you may have already had several sexual encounters; or maybe the temptation to try it is looming large; or maybe you are a virgin and simply long to one day experience IT. When any of us feels starved from a lack of attention and then a man gently touches us and tenderly speaks, we are drawn in emotionally. Face it—it feels good. All the layers of pleasing and meeting expectations crowd in; maybe you are ridiculed if you are still a virgin. According to *Sex and the City*, everybody's doing it—all the time and with many partners. Sex is the topic of nearly every conversation or the point or conclusion of most scenes. Is this even realistic, much less healthy?

It has become widely acceptable to have sex outside of marriage, and you may have never seriously thought otherwise. There is rarely an audible call to adults specifically to remain chaste. In the secular arena, that would sound ludicrous; few would consider it. From the pulpit, there is little acknowledgment that remaining pure is even a struggle, much less the admission that premarital sex is sin. I occasionally hear the admonition to marrieds to stay pure within their bond, but I rarely hear this call to singles.

I recently learned of two women, formerly staff members of a Christian organization, who are so discouraged by their singleness that they have laid aside their virginity for the physical affection of men. The desire to be desired, the ridicule about their virginity, and the hope for love have caused these

17

women to turn from long-held beliefs and convictions. Is there any problem with this? After all, such things happen every day, times have changed, and we are encouraged to follow suit.

We seem to forget that there will be some kind of impact on the heart and mind of a person who engages in sex. The question then stands: what is the impact outside of marriage? Compound one encounter with numerous partners and comparison or insecurity will undoubtedly take root, in addition to the increased risk of sexually transmitted diseases or pregnancy. We seem to ignore these realities all too often.

Have you ever weighed the advantages versus the disadvantages of premarital sex? Some people think just having that sexual experience is an advantage. There are, of course, beautiful aspects of sex—but in its proper context. Certainly many equate the act, the physicality, and the intimacy with love. But reflect on the emotions left to deal with when that man is gone. Mysteriously, when two people have sex, they are joined more intimately than by any other relationship or act. This is how it was meant to be. By stating that in marriage two become one flesh, God demonstrated the extremely high value he places on oneness. This bond in marriage and the symbolic metaphor it holds for the body of Christ is the highest approximation on this earth to the relationship within the Trinity. The Lord does not at all take this lightly; oneness is given tremendous priority in Scripture. Outside of marriage, sex cannot offer the same security and proper intimacy.

Bottom line: none of us can have sexual encounters and be whole, happy, and satisfied. We can deceive ourselves for a time, but cheapening sex cheapens us. The human heart left to its own lusts has an insatiable appetite for personal satisfaction or complete acceptance. Also, when we open ourselves vulnerably (and literally) to a man in that way and then he leaves, it rips out a part of our heart. It may not be visible at first, but over time, more is gone. I will never forget a skit I once saw at summer camp, highlighting scenes from preschool through high school in the life of a girl. She began as a precocious child, playing happily with a little orange (signifying her heart) that she had wrapped up in a blanket, pretending it was her baby; but then a neighbor grabbed the orange, bruising it. A few years later, she was teased about her outfit by some schoolmates as they dug into the orange. The skit finally culminated with a boyfriend who coaxed her into giving him her prized possession by fondly stroking it, until he got what he wanted, leaving her with the shreds of pulp and rind, barely reminiscent of the formerly beautiful and untouched orange.

If you are holding on to guilt about a sexual past, come to the Lord. Confess to him your sin and ask for his restoration in your heart and life. King David, whom the Lord declared a man after his own heart, found the forgiveness of the Lord after his adulterous affair with Bathsheba: "Cleanse me with hyssop, and I will be clean; wash me, and I will be whiter than snow" (Ps. 51:7).

The pressure is very great, coming from all angles: our personal passions that rage within us, the world that clamors right outside our door, men who would gladly spend a night of physical intoxication with us, and even the church that wonders why we are still single. But let us stand firm! In the name of Christ, "Submit yourselves, then, to God. Resist the devil, and he will flee from you" (James 4:7).

Expectations Dashed

We face expectations—almost daily, it seems—from family and married friends, who all mean well and desire our happiness. Their first solution for our struggles and lives is often marriage. (*Has this become our own "solution," too?*) Our world has convinced us that relationships will solve our problems—or at least lighten the load. The piece of news that seems to bring the most excitement to our family and friends is an announcement about a date or a boyfriend. But should this be the crux of life? In fact, relationships bring with them many *new* concerns. How many times, I wonder, does the married woman remember somewhat nostalgically the freedom and flexibility of the single life? As I observe my married sister with *four* children, I realize how tied down and consumed she is. Although the blessings of motherhood abound and it is good to be a mother, she will have the weighty responsibility of children at home for at least twenty-five years. She has virtually no time to call her own; free time is a memory of the past. (They always seem to leave this part out of the fairy tales and teen romances.) Be careful not to see marriage *only* as a blissful existence or an escape from loneliness.

The Comparison Game

I had never thought or cared much about dog shows until watching *Best in Show*.[4] Unscripted, it details, albeit humorously and possibly unrealistically, the lengths to which people will bend to come out ahead. In so many areas we compare our "dogs" with others, whether it be our lives, looks, or, yes, even our men. With past boyfriends, I (much to my chagrin) have stacked their qualities up against those of my friends' boyfriends. Also, I tend to pine away if several friends are dating and I am not. The question "What is wrong with me?" can too quickly creep into one's thoughts. Unfortunately, this is a battle that we must constantly wage in all areas. But be encouraged to stay in the battle. Don't give up! The Lord does

4. *Best in Show*, directed by Christopher Guest (Castle Rock Entertainment, 2000).

not compare us to others, and we are not expected to make comparisons, either.

The best combat I have found against the trap of the comparison game is to recognize that I am made in the image of God. We are all fearfully and wonderfully made (Ps. 139:14) for this time, place, and path. The load of pressure is lifted from our lives when we finally accept this fact.

I was recently in a women's Bible study that focused on Romans 12:2: "Do not conform any longer to the pattern of this world, but be transformed by the renewing of your mind." Quickly the discussion moved to the constant struggle faced by many in that room concerning image: how we look, how we cannot age gracefully in our society, and how we must be a certain size in order to live up to the world's standard. The entertainment industry has inundated the Western world with an ideology of beauty that is wreaking havoc on relationships, health, mental stability, and clear thinking. This may sound extreme, but think about the effects on relational expectations because of gorgeous bodies visually represented on TV, billboards, and movies. The beautiful people of the entertainment industry come to us in the form of manipulated and touched-up visual materials, the end product of which is often far different from the actual. It is no wonder many men and women aren't satisfied to date most people; no one can measure up.

While thinking on these realities, I read Psalm 27:2: "Evil men advance against me to devour my flesh." Do you see a correlation? Our flesh is, in a sense, being devoured. Individually we spend hundreds, maybe thousands, of dollars annually on our appearance: buying cosmetics to stop the wrinkles, hair color to hide the gray, and gorgeous clothes to make us look like the latest greatest model. Yet no matter how hard we resist, our bodies are aging and returning to dust. Regardless of how hard we try, we will never feel as though we measure up, and as a result, we are devoured in our inner being. I am reminded of Matthew 6:21: "For where your treasure is, there your heart will be also." Our treasure chests are filled with outward adornments that will rot and fade away instead of lasting for eternity.

Pursuing the world's standards of beauty keeps our eyes on the world and off the Lord. We are held captive by these images and driven to somehow keep up. Much of our time is consumed with making a good impression through our looks and outward presentation—perchance to catch a man. We have been imprisoned in darkness by the one who "masquerades as an angel of light" (2 Cor. 11:14). Our striving for beauty has truly entrapped us and sent us on an unending quest for an unattainable ideal. We have forgotten the inner individual and the work of redemption that the Lord desires in our lives. He came "to proclaim freedom for the captives and release from darkness for the prisoners, . . . [and] to bestow on them a crown of beauty instead of ashes, . . . and a garment of praise instead of a spirit of despair" (Isa. 61:1, 3). The Lord does not intend for us to be trapped by the world's requirements for appearance. Our Father longs to crown us with his beauty—which is based on his work alone and frees us from ceaseless striving. His crown of beauty will never fade and is defined by his everlasting standards, not those of this world that will turn to dust.

Decide now to step out of the rat race of measuring up. Our existence or worth cannot be justified by any of the world's means or accomplishments.

If Only . . .

"If only I were married!" Unfortunately, this mind-set is the engine that operates a vicious cyclical machine that will quickly entrap us. It begins early on—whenever we become discontent with our present situation.

Many of us have believed that *if only* we were married, we would no longer be lonely or battle depression or feel unloved or . . . . Every stage of life can become ensnared by *if only*. Once one is married, the cry is, "*If only* I had a child!" Then, when the child is born or adopted, the parent dreams, "*If only* we had a larger house." In the new house, after more diapers and temper tantrums than imaginable, the outburst of desperation may be, "*If only* my baby were of school age!" And the cycle continues. If we were to link all our *if only* statements in life, we would probably have a chain long enough to choke out all hope of satisfaction. We must stop this cycle *now*, before we continue to spiral downward into a life of discontentment.

We must also remember that beyond the *if only*, when that goal is attained, the reality is often much different from the dream. William Makepeace Thackeray in *Vanity Fair* captures the awakening to reality for Amelia, the supporting female character, merely nine days after her wedding to the man of her dreams:

> What a gulf lay between her and that past life. She could look back to it from her present standing-place, and contemplate, almost as another being, the young unmarried girl absorbed in her love, having no eyes but for one special object . . .—her whole heart and thoughts bent on the accomplishment of one desire . . . : as if, once landed in the marriage country, all were green and pleasant there: and wife and husband had nothing to do but to link each other's arms together, and wander gently downwards towards old age in happy and perfect fruition.[5]

5. William Makepeace Thackeray, *Vanity Fair* (New York: Random House, 2001), 268–69.

Loneliness arises even in marriage. Many married women struggle with bouts of depression and often feel unloved. The grass is *not* always greener on the other side; it is only a different kind of grass.

I Just Can't Believe!

At the other end of the spectrum from *if only* is *it never will be*. In a quest to avoid being consumed with thoughts of marriage, we can err on the side of hope forgotten. I have found myself at times so anxious to *not* be disappointed that I have tended to block out all desires for matrimony. Instead, we still can genuinely hope that God will bring a mate—believing even if we cannot see the way. I love Paul's description of Abraham in Romans 4:18: "Against all hope, Abraham in hope believed." We would do well to follow this bold determination to believe God's faithfulness against the odds—regardless of whether or not we will marry. Remember, however, the necessary balance between hoping in God's provision along with contentment in our present situation.

The dream of attraction can be frustrating when you find no one to whom to be attracted or, on the other end of the spectrum, you feel that no one will ever be attracted to you. Do you struggle to believe that God will ever bring along your husband—one you will love and desire as a partner?

As Abraham looked at the reality of his life juxtaposed with God's promise to him to be made "into a great nation" (Gen. 12:2), he asked, "O Sovereign LORD, what can you give me since I remain childless . . . ?" (15:2). The key for us is Abraham's address of God: he recognizes God as Adonai Jehovah—the One who is over all, the Lord who set the stars in the heavens and arranged each molecule in the universe, he who ordains all that comes to pass. When Abraham believed God's word regardless of the circumstances visible before him,

God "credited it to him as righteousness" (15:6). He is later included in the book of Hebrews' "Hall of Faith" "because he considered him faithful who had made the promise" (Heb. 11:11).

Even though we don't receive specific promises from God for every instance—for example, that we will marry—we know that he will provide for our needs, that he will always protect us, and that he offers complete freedom in Christ. Also, if he desires for us to marry, it *will* happen because God is sovereign. Have you ceased to believe these truths? God might be saying in this instance, "You of little faith" (Matt. 16:8). As the disciples did, we, too, forget the many past ways in which the Lord has provided loaves of bread and fish to feed thousands. His blessings to us have been abundant. Why do we doubt that he can move heaven and earth to bring our husbands to us? He created the universe out of nothing (Heb. 11:3). God's plan cannot be thwarted. Remember, though, that it will be in his timing if it will be at all. And whatever his plan, it is best.

You might have believed the lie that since many marriages will end in divorce anyway, why even hope? This fatalistic attitude can surely rob us of our energy and any zest for life. It also dangles us precariously somewhere between an embittered single woman and a hard-nosed, independent feminist. Bottom line: God has instituted marriage and it is good, so it is a valid life stage about which we can pray and hope—without being consumed by these thoughts. Hope most fervently *in the Lord!*

The Truth

These are some of the messages Satan has used to deceive us so that our perception of reality is distorted. But there is a true Story beyond every earthly tale; there is a greater Story behind our individual stories. It began before time, and all of history is marching toward its grand climax. This Story was birthed in the heart of God and declared through his Word, which is

> most of all a Story. It's an adventure story about a young Hero who comes from a far country to win back his lost treasure. It's a love story about a brave Prince who leaves his palace, his throne—everything—to rescue the one he loves. It's like the most wonderful of fairy tales that has come true in real life!
>
> You see, the best thing about this Story is—it's true.[6]

Even if we truly want to place our trust in the Lord as our heavenly Prince and Rescuer, we still live in this world! How do we combat the strong messages that constantly bombard our thoughts and lives?

Following the example of the psalmist who declared, "I will set before my eyes no vile thing" (Ps. 101:3), we can monitor the images and ideas that we allow to enter our minds and hearts. Many times we move through our days without any precaution regarding the information that bombards us daily.

Instead, there is a better way and a single focus that we can pursue: "One thing I ask of the LORD, this is what I seek: that I may dwell in the house of the LORD all the days of my life, to gaze upon the beauty of the LORD and to seek him in his temple" (Ps. 27:4).

Dwelling in the house of the Lord will not, of course, be a physical reality until we reach heaven. But figuratively, we can dwell, rest, and exist in the Lord's presence. This may

6. Sally Lloyd-Jones, *The Jesus Storybook Bible* (Grand Rapids: Zonderkidz, 2007), 17.

seem rather ethereal to some of you, but pray for his constant presence with you and truly seek him. We cannot just hope that this will happen and wish that we would no longer be caught up in the worldly races toward beauty and acceptance. We must seek the Lord with all our heart, soul, mind, and strength. When you walk outside, recognize and thank him as Creator of the natural surroundings. Look at yourself in light of how *he* sees you: as a beloved, beautiful daughter.

"Gaze upon the beauty of the LORD." Rest in the peace of that concept for a moment. Try to grasp what this means. The Lord is beautiful—everything that is lovely, good, and perfect.

> For as God is infinitely the greatest being, so he is . . . infinitely the most beautiful and excellent: and all the beauty to be found throughout the whole creation, is but the reflection of diffused beams of that Being who hath an infinite fullness of brightness and glory.[7]

We can cease striving and delight in the Lord's attractiveness. Remember also that we have been created in his image, so he has imputed his beauty to us in some way.

I love the determination of the psalmist in this verse: "My heart says of you, 'Seek his face!' Your face, LORD, I will seek" (Ps. 27:8). A definite decision and continual action must take place. I think of a child who grabs her daddy's face, both hands exuberantly cupping his two cheeks, puts herself within a few inches, and looks intently into his two eyes. Stop gazing in the mirror and gaze instead into the face of the Father.

We must always seek the Lord, for Satan attacks from every angle. In the wake of David's encroaching enemy, he declared:

7. Jonathan Edwards, *A Jonathan Edwards Reader*, ed. John E. Smith et al. (New Haven: Yale University Press, 2003), 252.

"Though an army besiege me, my heart will not fear; though war break out against me, even then will I be confident" (Ps. 27:3). We, too, can have this confidence, especially as we seek the Lord and gaze upon his beauty, reminding our hearts of the truths of his Word and our standing in his eyes. He looks at us with eyes of love and full acceptance because of Christ.

One of the most prevalent roadblocks to contentment is that we do not believe in God's goodness. If we truly believe that God is good in the midst of *every* circumstance, then we can trust that we are in the situation that is the best. Romans 8:28 says that "in all things God works for the good of those who love him, who have been called according to his purpose." Nothing in this passage qualifies "all things" as being only spiritual, familial, or related to any other one circumstance. So it must describe *all* things. This means that God is working for our good through our jobs, in the families he has given us, where we are living, and, yes, even through our lives as singles. This is not to say that all circumstances are good; they are what they are. But God works in all of them for our good.

The conclusion of Psalm 27 is: "I am still confident of this: I will see the goodness of the LORD in the land of the living. Wait for the LORD; be strong and take heart and wait for the LORD" (Ps. 27:13–14). Do you grasp the fullness of these verses? The outcome is not clear, but the confidence in the Lord is solid. The Lord's goodness will come.

Meditation Moments

1. Do you have difficulty accepting singleness? Do you feel discontent and joyless? Explore the reasons why.
2. Do you long for contentment? How do you seek it? Consider whether the Lord is challenging you to change your perspective on contentment.

3. How have you been longing for a fairy tale?
4. Look back over the struggles listed in this chapter. Do any of them resonate with your own struggles? If so, how do they play out in your life?
5. Contemplate other areas of struggle for you regarding singleness. Process through them; ask questions; pray through them.
6. How have you bought into the lies that are infiltrating our society? What does the Lord say about you? (Read: Ps. 23:5-6; Isa. 43:1-3; 1 John 3:1)

2 Why Do Bad Things Happen? *Why We Suffer*

● ● ● ● ● ● ● ● ● ● ● ● ● ● ● ● ●

The Age-Old Question

The trip to the greeting-card store for a friend's birthday is generally predictable: many lost minutes searching for the perfect card, only to settle for a less-than-adequate sentiment on the value of friendship, caring, and so on. Every few years, though, we actually find that one-in-a-million card that sums it all up. This was my experience several years ago; so fantastic was the card, I still have not been able to part with it. It was one of those that makes you laugh out loud in the middle of the card aisle at the local store. If only I could include the illustration, you might laugh, too, but the sarcastic humor will be clear regardless:

> I'm searching for that one right person who's different from all the rest . . . [*Open card*] . . . One who will go out with me.[1]

1. Leslie Moak Murray, www.murrayslaw.com.

It is humor like this that I think we need at times to lighten up our outlook. Maybe you are able to laugh at this sentiment, but it could also bring you to tears because it's too close to your heartfelt emotions.

As the months and years pile up without a marriage pro-posal, we can feel overwhelmed with loneliness, thoughts of inadequacy, and isolation. I have spoken with several women who think they would be happy if simply *one* guy would call for a date. We find ourselves stuck in our jobs, dissatisfied with the place in which we live, and tired of yet again rent-ing a sappy romance movie to watch with a girlfriend—or alone. Often, we may view our lives as a dead-end street to nowhere. We hurt; we struggle. An ache gnaws deep inside of us, and a longing is unfulfilled. Why? This question has taken me on a journey to discover the extent of our experience in light of the overarching suffering in the world and the proper responses to it.

Before delving into this topic, we must acknowledge that our emotions are real. God himself has given us the wonderful ability to experience intensely, and we should never squelch our emotions. The key is to be honest with each other and feel deeply before the Lord, allowing him to hear our cries and heal our hurts. If we are in despair, he does not wish for us to stay there. "Cast your cares on the LORD and he will sustain you; he will never let the righteous fall" (Ps. 55:22). This exhortation is not a lofty expression from a nameless, detached voice, but from David, one of the most passionate and prolific psalmists. We would do well to often consider the Psalms, of which John Calvin, a great theologian of the sixteenth century, said:

> There is not an emotion of which anyone can be conscious that is not here represented as in a mirror. Or rather, the Holy

Spirit has here drawn . . . all the griefs, sorrows, fears, doubts, hopes, cares, perplexities, in short, all the distracting emotions with which the minds of men are wont to be agitated.[2]

The Psalms lend poignant words to the anguish of our souls, and more importantly, are contained in the very Word of God. They provide comfort for us in suffering.

What is the end assessment of Psalm 55? "But as for me, I trust in you" (Ps. 55:23). Is this our own final analysis? Take time to meditate on this psalm. Bring your broken heart, questions, doubts, and frustrations to the Lord, the Healer of our souls.

Paradise Lost[3]

Struggle is unavoidable in this life. Philosophers, parents, intellectuals, store clerks—all kinds of people wrestle with this reality, its source, and its implications. One of the most frequent questions—"Why do bad things happen to good people?"—has no doubt been a cry of our own hearts, for it is hard for us to accept suffering, especially in the lives of people who seem to be upright or innocent. Of course, the accurate questions, in light of Romans 3:23 ("all have sinned and fall short of the glory of God"), should be, "Why does anything good happen to bad people?" and "Who are the 'bad' people?" This has been true since that first fateful day in the garden of Eden. Adam and Eve severed their intimate relationship with God through sin; they wanted to satisfy their desire for the one forbidden fruit and gain all knowledge. They wanted to be gods themselves instead of enjoying fellowship with the one true God.

2. John Calvin, *Commentary on the Psalms* (Grand Rapids: Baker Book House, 1979), xxxvi.
3. Title borrowed from John Milton, *Paradise Lost*, 1667.

Sin brought a curse on the world so that perfection was tarnished. Scripture says the whole creation is groaning as in the pains of childbirth (Rom. 8:22). Original sin reaches into every area of life, including health, aging, and finances. Remember the pain at losing a loved one; think about the devastation of the recent hurricanes, tsunamis, and fires; recall to mind the emaciated face of a starving child. These are realities because of a fallen world, bringing suffering that cannot be reasoned away. There are times of mourning and times that call for mercy.

Our Plans versus His Plans

Another reason we struggle is that our lives have not turned out as we planned. Remember the dream: after college meet Prince Charming, marry, and have two beautiful children by age 27? Regardless of your past or present expectations, do not allow them to dictate or cloud the possibilities and potential that God has for your life. Remember that human perceptions don't line up with God's view. He is constantly confounding the wisdom and philosophies of the world—those stating that the powerful and beautiful people are to be exalted, for example. He chose Jacob, the younger, over Esau; he told Hosea to take for a wife a prostitute who would be unfaithful to him, in order to illustrate Israel's unfaithfulness to Yahweh God. Furthermore, consider the mothers in the lineage of Christ: Leah, the unloved one; Tamar, who birthed a child through the adulterous action of Judah; Ruth, who was a Moabite, one outside the people of Israel; Bathsheba, whom David had wronged through adultery. These do not seem to be likely women through whom God would work, and yet he did! The clear and resounding implication is that he will proceed with his plans, not capitulate to our expectations.

34

I have always been drawn to the story of Joseph, probably because it is such an amazing account of restoration and ascent from rags to riches. In a sense, it is a picture of the work of redemption that God brings in our lives: taking us from being proud and self-reliant individuals through the crucible to being servants to him and others.

It doesn't take long to read Joseph's story in Genesis 37–50, but in reality the bird's-eye view we are given spanned many years. At age seventeen, when Joseph was sold into slavery by his very own brothers, he undoubtedly struggled immensely, wondering about the plan for his life. Was he to be separated from his family only to die a slave in a foreign land? His life continued as a roller-coaster ride for the next twenty-two years—through service to a rich official where he earned respect, only to be unjustly thrown in jail for two years, until he was elevated to the second-highest position in the land.

Joseph was thirty-nine when, after years of uncertainty, his life started to make some sense. Until then, it might have seemed that there was no purpose in being apart from family. Joseph could never have guessed during this desert time in Egypt the overarching plan of God, who sovereignly weaves even bad events and decisions into his good plan. Maybe we should more readily abandon our feverish search for the point to the circumstances in our lives, including singleness. We probably won't figure it out until years later—or even until eternity! God could have sent Joseph easily and directly to Egypt as a stellar economist and leader without all the seeming detours and trials. But then Joseph would have been prideful and selfish, his family would not have been reconciled, and they would not have relocated to Egypt, where God cultivated his nation, Israel. As a result of God implementing his plans, Israel became a people set apart unto Yahweh God.

35

One of the most beautiful verses in all of Scripture is found at the end of the account of Joseph, when he speaks to his brothers: "You intended to harm me, but God intended it for good *to accomplish what is now being done, the saving of many lives*" (Gen. 50:20). God has a different plan from ours, and often this plan, though *good*, involves suffering.

Do you struggle to keep worldly concerns from extinguishing your hope in God's higher plan? Dr. Bryan Chapell, president of Covenant Theological Seminary, beautifully broaches this subject in his article "Rainbow Chasing":

> Even as I chase rainbows I know that I will never see a whole one with my feet on the earth. I will see the bow, at most, from horizon to horizon, in a wonderful arch. But from earth's vantage I will never see a complete rainbow, the huge circle that it is, where God has completed the whole thing. Earth always gets in the way![4]

Doesn't that sum up the real frustration? Even if we want to believe in God's overarching plan, earth often gets in the way. Let us pray for God to remind us of his perspective and grasp all we can of his sovereignty with eyes wide open, knowing without a doubt the good plans he has for us. Don't let your world get in the way!

God's Crucible

I often think of Joni Eareckson Tada, who was paralyzed in her teens as the result of a horrible diving injury. God has used her *because* of her paralysis and testimony to touch millions of people worldwide. Her story should be an inspiration to live boldly and passionately for God with the tools

4. Bryan Chapell, "Rainbow Chasing," *Covenant Magazine* (Summer 2003): 5.

and weaknesses he has given us. She has chosen to live as Paul, boasting

> all the more gladly about my weaknesses, so that Christ's power may rest on me. That is why, for Christ's sake, I delight in weaknesses, in insults, in hardships, in persecutions, in difficulties. For when I am weak, then I am strong. (2 Cor. 12:9-10)

A third cause for struggle, which Scripture highlights in several instances, is when suffering is laid on a person *by God*, apart from a specific sin. Jeremiah, author of two books of Scripture, is often called the "weeping prophet" because his life was ridden with affliction as he brought the Lord's word to the Israelites. King David spent much of his adult life hiding from those who sought to kill him. And of course, Jesus himself was "despised and rejected by men, a man of sorrows, and familiar with suffering" (Isa. 53:3). This theology can be extremely difficult to accept unless we first believe unstintingly in the love of God for us. Then and only then can we begin to understand that the trials he puts into our lives are in order to shape us, to woo us continually back to himself, and to work his redemption through us. This truth is illustrated in Psalm 66:8-12:

> Praise our God, O peoples,
>> let the sound of his praise be heard;
> he has preserved our lives
>> and kept our feet from slipping.
> For you, O God, tested us;
>> you refined us like silver.
> You brought us into prison
>> and laid burdens on our backs.

You let men ride over our heads;
    we went through fire and water,
    but you brought us to a place of abundance.

A silversmith must submit unrefined silver to intense heat in order to remove the impurities. The result is a beautiful product worth a great sum. Our heavenly Father is the silversmith in our lives, standing over the heat, carefully and watchfully holding us in the fire for just the right amount of time. He knows how to make a perfect and priceless piece of silver. His love is so great that he will not be content with ordinary metal; he is making a masterpiece out of your life! We can deduce from this image that our Lord is actively and intimately involved in the process, not far removed. He himself is holding us over the fire, feeling the heat along with us. Did you notice in the passage above that the Lord himself brought his people into prison?

In the following letter to her daughter, Sarah Edwards displayed similar hope in the Lord in the midst of enduring the loss of her husband and well-known preacher, Jonathan Edwards:

> My very dear child!
> What shall I say? A holy and good God has covered us with a dark cloud. O that we may kiss the rod, and lay our hands on our mouths! The Lord has done it. He has made me adore his goodness, that we had [your father] so long. But my God lives; and He has my heart. O what a legacy my husband, and your father, has left us! We are all given to God; and there I am, and love to be.
> Your affectionate mother,
> Sarah Edwards[5]

5. Letter from Sarah Edwards, wife of Jonathan Edwards, to their daughter, Esther, 1758, in *A God-Entranced Vision of All Things: The Legacy of Jonathan Edwards*, ed. John Piper and Justin Taylor (Wheaton, IL: Crossway, 2004), 75.

When I see lives such as these lived, albeit with suffering, before God with great praise, trust, and reliance, *I* am encouraged and God is glorified.

Miss Stacy, in one of my favorite films, *Anne of Green Gables*, encourages Anne with these words: "These trials and tribulations that pop up in our lives . . . serve a very useful purpose: they build character—as long as we can hold on to the lessons we've learned from our mistakes."[6] This vaguely reminiscent spiritual theme finds its fullness and roots in the Word of God.

Proved Genuine

God also allows testing in our lives to prove us genuinely his. In Job 1:6–12, we read a discourse between God and Satan concerning the great prosperity of Job, a God-fearing man. "But stretch out your hand and strike everything he has, and he will surely curse you to your face" (v. 11). God allows intense suffering to come into his servant Job's life, and because he is the Lord's, Job does not curse God. Yes, the pain is searing and almost unbearable, but Satan is proved wrong.

> Now for a little while you may have had to suffer grief in all kinds of trials. These have come so that your faith—of greater worth than gold, which perishes even though refined by fire—may be proved genuine and may result in praise, glory and honor when Jesus Christ is revealed. (1 Peter 1:6–7)

Has our faith, in fact, been "proved genuine"? Regardless of the circumstances of our lives (e.g., financial troubles, loneliness, health issues), we still have "a living hope through the resurrection of Jesus Christ from the dead, and

6. *Anne of Green Gables*, directed by Kevin Sullivan (Toronto: CityTV, 1985).

into an inheritance that can never perish, spoil or fade"
(1 Peter 1:3–4). The suffering of the saints allows God's
redemptive work to be seen all the more. As individuals
continue to live by Christ alone and praise him in the midst
of pain and trial, he is glorified. The Huaorani people of
Ecuador, who killed the missionary Jim Elliot, were won
over to Christ through the faithful service of his widow,
Elisabeth Elliot. She had suffered greatly by the hand of
this tribe, but she continued following her Lord by living
among these people.

The apostle Paul, too, remained steadfast against seemingly
insurmountable odds, as seen in 2 Corinthians 4:8–12:

> We are hard pressed on every side, but not crushed; perplexed,
> but not in despair; persecuted, but not abandoned; struck
> down, but not destroyed. We always carry around in our
> body the death of Jesus, so that the life of Jesus may also be
> revealed in our body. For we who are alive are always being
> given over to death for Jesus' sake, so that his life may be
> revealed in our mortal body. So then, death is at work in us,
> but life is at work in you.

Christ, when tempted by Satan, was offered all the riches
of the world, but without the suffering of the cross. Pastor Mo
Leverett, founder of Desire Street Ministries in New Orleans,
observes:

> I am convinced that the same temptation Jesus faced is what
> is being presented to the American evangelical church of
> today—for you to accept a form of religion, a version of
> Christianity, without the cross; that you can reach the heights
> of Christian maturity without suffering redemptively for the

sake of others, that you can see the spread of the Gospel where there is no suffering.[7]

It is impossible for us to share in Christ's and others' sufferings without enduring suffering ourselves.

Whatever you are facing, remember Romans 8:35–39 (quoting Ps. 44:22):

> Who shall separate us from the love of Christ? Shall trouble or hardship or persecution or famine or nakedness or danger or sword? As it is written: "For your sake we face death all day long; we are considered as sheep to be slaughtered." No, in all these things we are more than conquerors through him who loved us. For I am convinced that neither death nor life, neither angels nor demons, neither the present nor the future, nor any powers, neither height nor depth, nor anything else in all creation, will be able to separate us from the love of God that is in Christ Jesus our Lord.

May these many Scriptures speak loudly into our lives. The Word understands suffering, resonates deeply with our pain, and offers the only true hope for this world. Turn to the Word, and find life in Christ in the midst of suffering.

Meditation Moments

1. During trials, have you ever been able to say with the psalmist in Psalm 55:23, "But as for me, I trust in you"? Why is this trust so hard? What does such trust require of us?
2. What do you really believe about suffering and its potential in your life? How can we as individuals change our

7. Mo Leverett, sermon at The Covenant Presbyterian Church (St. Louis, November 17, 2002).

perspective so that we anticipate suffering? Is it possible to welcome and even embrace suffering?

3. What are some of the struggles you face? Do you struggle with the struggles themselves? (In other words, how is it difficult to accept struggles in our lives?)

4. Meditate on the life of Christ, especially as seen in Isaiah 53. How can looking at Christ's struggles help us in our own struggles?

5. Take time to study each of the passages suggested in this chapter.

3   Call It What It Is!

●●●●●●●●●●●●●●●●

WHEN WE SUFFER, we may grudgingly conclude that it is allowed by a sovereign God. Or in catastrophic events such as Hurricane Katrina or 9/11, it is easy to blame others for the horrible conditions prevalent in our world. But do we ever ponder whether we ourselves are culpable for any of the pain in our relationships and life? We must recognize that we contribute to the brokenness around us.

The Plank in the Eye

Jesus warns us in Matthew 7:3, "Why do you look at the speck of sawdust in your brother's eye and pay no attention to the plank in your own eye?" So often our actions and speech are no different from those of Adam and Eve, who were quick to shift blame. If we think we personally would have responded better than the first humans did, take into account how often we fight God or strike out on our own when we cannot yet see his plan around the bend or how quickly we give in to our desires. We eat forbidden fruit daily—when we doubt God, when we are deceived, or when we want to take situations into our own hands and try to be God. Wrongs against each other or toward God build walls between relationships and do great damage against mankind.

Recently I have heard a lot of grumbling from singles within the church. Both men and women are frustrated with the opposite sex, are discontented regarding the low percentage of dating, and call the leadership into question because of perceived inaction or lack of attention toward the "plight of the single."

Singles can often fall into a trap of ignoring personal responsibility and blaming others. When we as single women complain against the church or our brothers, the obvious deduction is that we are single because of them. This view completely negates any contribution of our own past negative responses toward men and choices we have made, not to mention God's hand in our lives.

For example, when we berate a man to our girlfriends, we are damaging their opinion of him. Maybe you happen to dislike the way he talks or how he asked you out for a date. Does this warrant gabbing to your friends? I myself am the most guilty of this and have found myself relaying a particular instance to a girlfriend—of course with the most dramatic presentation possible in order to get the largest reaction. To what gain was this? The expense was the Christian man's reputation. I guarantee that he will have no chance at a date with my friend now. And heaven wept. We women too often think we are the only ones who pay for the predicament of singleness.

Before blaming our Christian brothers for not treating us as we would like or not being the perfect God we want in human form, let us consider first whether we are without fault. There are enough victims in our society; let's not join the bandwagon.

Our own sin also distances us from our heavenly Father and clouds our vision of his sovereignty in our lives. His holiness cannot be in the presence of sin—so how can we pretend that he can abide with us in the act of sin? Ask him to reveal to you how you have grieved him. If we don't ask, he will eventually intercede and bring us to our knees before him. Often he will pull our distractions away from us or allow suffering. This is *not* because he is a mean God; but he is a jealous lover. We cannot understand this until we begin to grasp the full extent of his passion for us. Search the Old Testament for references of his abiding love and how he pursued his children, Israel. Time and time again, they turned from him to other gods. At times, they were so stubborn that he disciplined them—by sending them into exile, for example. When we complain that God was unfair in this action, ponder the hundreds of years of his patience! By turning our backs on God and living our lives apart from him, we are missing out on his spiritual blessings. He wants abundance for us.

One More Invitation!

Do you remember a month in the past when you received multiple invitations to weddings or baby showers? How did you feel? I will admit that several years ago I decided on the day of a friend's wedding that I just couldn't go. It seemed too hard; I didn't want to cry at one more wedding because I was not the bride. And yet Scripture says to rejoice with those who rejoice. That must not apply to this situation, however, right?

Well, actually, it does. So why was I unable to rejoice in this Christian wedding? Because deep in my heart at that moment I longed for what my friend was attaining that day; I was dissatisfied with still being single. I can try to sugarcoat the emotions and motives, but, quite honestly, at the core was *envy*. A very small word, but one rife with negativity and destructive power. Be convinced by these words from James 3:14–16:

> If you harbor bitter envy and selfish ambition in your hearts, do not boast about it *or deny the truth*. Such "wisdom" does not come down from heaven but is earthly, unspiritual, of the devil. For where you have envy and selfish ambition, there you find disorder and *every evil* practice.

Please believe that I do not mean to discount the real emotions of sadness that we may experience at not yet having a mate or children. But emotions can lead to temptation, which can grow into sin if left unchecked. In truth, can any of us deny that we have harbored envy? Regarding desire for marriage, may we bow before God for mercy and grace! Envy deadens our lives and robs us of joy. It creeps in like a vine and will eventually choke out the life inside.

Several years ago, I moved to the same city as my sister and her husband and kids—expressly to be near family. They graciously allowed me to live with them for a time. First I noticed the nice furniture and established home; then I observed all the family heirlooms that my sister had incorporated into her home; before long I found myself almost looking for things she had that I didn't have. By the time I moved out, my heart had become so hard and bitter that I almost hated being with my sister. Envy had filled me like a disease and was eating away at my relationship with one I dearly love. I could not enjoy the time with the family or their hospitality toward me. It took me several years of praying through those feelings and confessing my sin before God restored our relationship. Envy is a hideous sin. I have seen its sad effects in my own life. It has made me unable at various times to rejoice with family and friends at the good work of God in their lives.

To spell it out plainly, when you want something that belongs to someone else and that desire adversely affects you, you are envious. We can spot this sin when we believe that nothing we have is good enough and then we can't enjoy anything.

It is amazing how quickly envy creeps in! Allow me to share a few thoughts captured in my journal from a past day in my life:

> Yesterday was a beautiful 60-degree November day in Manhattan. I have just relocated here by some amazing movements by God, I've started meeting many wonderful people, and yet I found myself noticing all the couples walking by me. Before long I was feeling lonely and almost a little depressed. This in the midst of ALL God has done recently! I am obviously right where he wants me and he has provided abundantly more than I could ask or imagine, and yet I was envious of what I didn't have!

How ungrateful we are! Our salvation should be enough; it should be our glory, our joy, our abundance. We have every spiritual blessing in Christ (Eph. 1:3); we are chosen (v. 4); we are adopted as children because of his predestining love (v. 5); he has given us his glorious grace (v. 6) and redemption through his blood (v. 7); and he has made known to us the mystery of his will: to bring all things under Christ (v. 10). Do you understand the wealth we have in Christ? His blessings are abundant!

Yet we forget.

The psalmist in the face of envy declared, "My feet had almost slipped . . . for I envied . . . the prosperity of the wicked" (Ps. 73:2–3). He described his desire for prosperity, a struggle-free life, health, strength, and freedom from burdens and ills (vv. 4–5). But that led him to pride, violence, iniquity, evil conceit, scoffing, and malice (vv. 6–12). Is this really what we want?

Even though this psalmist refers directly to his envy of the ungodly, we are not exempt when we covet something belonging to a godly friend. The effects are the same; *nothing* is right or good to covet.

The truth I can speak to the Lord is this: "I am always with you; you hold me by my right hand. . . . Earth has nothing I desire besides you. . . . It is good to be near God" (Ps. 73:23, 25, 28).

What do you desire?

De-si-i-i-i-i-re[1]

Envy leads us right into another sin that traps us with regard to singleness and marriage: idolatry. Single women can place marriage on a pedestal where God never intended it to be. Even married women can fall into the same trap. This form of idolatry can lead to dissatisfaction because we worship a fantasized picture of marriage or a man never meant to be in the place of God. Additionally, the man you may marry probably will be vastly different from your idol.

If I am unhappy as a single, there is a good chance that I'll be unhappy as a married woman. *Why?* I have a specific picture of a man in mind as well as ideas of how marriage will satisfy. But marriage in the flesh to an actual man is bound to disappoint me at times and not meet my high expectations. Only Christ will fully satisfy. He has already sacrificed all for me and pursues me daily. His love will never fail. He wants the best for me 100 percent of the time. He is never seeking his own good at my expense. Unfortunately, spouses in their humanity will not always seek the other's interests first.

1. "Desire," by U2 (Paul Hewson, Dave Evans, Adam Clayton, and Larry Mullen; Island Records, 1988).

If you marry, continually surrender your husband to God and recognize the Lord alone as God; chances are, your idol husband will come crashing down soon enough because you will place him far above, where God alone can dwell. And in truth, as one of my pastors, Dr. Keller, has preached, "If we have an ultimate passion other than God, we will eventually lose that thing."[2]

I must mention an area of concern as we ponder idolatry in light of marriage: it is possible to guard ourselves too much against desiring marriage—to the point of fearing a relationship with a man altogether and fleeing from the possibility of love. This is *not* good!

> Love anything and your heart will be wrung and possibly broken. If you want to make sure of keeping it intact you must give it to no one, not even an animal. Wrap it carefully round with hobbies and little luxuries; avoid all entanglements. Lock it up safe in the casket or coffin of your selfishness. But in that casket—safe, dark, motionless, airless—it will change. It will not be broken; it will become unbreakable, impenetrable, irredeemable.[3]

We must maintain an open heart toward marriage, recognizing it as a gift of God, without placing it on a pedestal. Obviously, we need God's grace and guidance because this can be quite a balancing act. I personally have sometimes resisted the idea of marriage more than I have been open to considering or welcoming a man into my life. I have struggled with how a man can be my love while the Lord is my ultimate life. And yet this is a God-ordained possibility! This reality comes, I

2. Timothy Keller, *Sermon Series on Proverbs* (New York: Redeemer Presbyterian Church, Fall 2004).
3. C. S. Lewis, *The Inspirational Writings of C. S. Lewis* (New York: Inspirational Press, 1994), 278.

believe, as marriage often drives two humans once again to the cross. It is one of the many mysteries and blessings of life.

The "I-Complex"

Perhaps, instead of placing another person on the throne meant for God alone, we have lifted up ourselves. This grievous sin pulls our focus away from caring for others and loving God. We spend so much time worrying about ourselves and our own pleasure or pain that we forget that there are other people in the world. This tendency begins at birth because of our sin nature. It is not a learned behavior; we want to be gods. In the nursery or on the playground, observe children who will pitch a fit if another child has the coveted toy or swing of the day. Parents spend painstaking hours—even years—training their children to share.

This part of our nature does not bode well for relationships. If we are honest with ourselves, we will recognize that the desire to personally be happy and secure will easily trump our service and self-sacrifice toward others. Think about how we bulldoze over people and worthy priorities to get what we want—sometimes even to get a certain someone who has struck our fancy.

Remember King David, who lusted after and got what he wanted (Bathsheba) at the expense of his and her purity and the life of his friend, Bathsheba's husband. David's determination to obtain his desire led to the death of a friend and of his own child, as well as many other consequences and pain. Speaking specifically of marriage, although this is a worthy pursuit, we need to seriously question *why* we want to get married instead of blindly demanding that it happen. Is it only to fulfill us personally? Many have a "what's in it for me?" mentality instead of seeking a life of service to the other.

Fear

Another struggle that we must confront as single women is fear. For years, I felt vulnerable to harm (physical and sexual) simply for being a woman. I have had to learn to trust my life and care to the Lord. Also, I think there is uneasiness about providing endlessly for ourselves. As singles we need to be independent, self-providing humans, of course, but most of my friends long to not have to carry this weight alone. I believe these insecurities arise in part because we were created to be helpmates, to have someone watching over us and caring for us. In our society, though, we often feel as though we are pushed out of the nest without another home into which to fall. I love the illustration painted for us in Deuteronomy 32:11, in which the Lord is "like an eagle that stirs up its nest and hovers over its young, that spreads its wings to catch them and carries them on its pinions." In order to teach its young to "soar on wings like eagles" (Isa. 40:31), the parent eagle pushes its young out of the nest of comfort—but then mightily swoops down to lift them up on its strong wings, having allowed them to fall only as long as is necessary for their growth and development.

Do we believe the Lord will take care of us, as the eagle cares for its young? Scripture contains countless examples of his protection of his children. Consider Exodus 14:13, in which Moses said to the Israelites facing the vast Egyptian army: "Do not be afraid. Stand firm and you will see the deliverance the LORD *will* bring *you* today." Do you fear having enough money to pay the bills? The Lord will provide. Do you fear growing old on your own? The Lord is your portion (Ps. 73:26). "The LORD [not the knowledge of the future, or a mate, but the Lord] is my light and my salvation—whom shall I fear? The LORD is the stronghold of my life—of whom shall I be afraid?" (Ps. 27:1).

We need not fear the future and what it holds, for God holds the future.

A Tree Planted by the Water

I wish I could declare that the sins and failings mentioned in this chapter, now that I have recognized them, no longer plague me. In truth, it is more likely that we all need to *daily* confess these tendencies to God, praying for "an undivided heart, that I may fear your name" (Ps. 86:11).

What is the solution for our tendencies to sin? To be confronted with our Lord. May we declare with David's Psalm 63:2–4:

> I have seen you in the sanctuary
> > and beheld your power and your glory.
> Because your love is better than life,
> > my lips will glorify you.
> I will praise you as long as I live,
> > and in your name I will lift up my hands.

The Lord, in turn, will inform and direct us in all our relationships. We can also be greatly encouraged: "Resist the devil, and he will flee from you" (James 4:7). Hope is not lost. Victory is within reach! God desires for us to experience restoration and fullness.

Let us no longer fear the future or our circumstances; may we no longer desire the life and possessions of others; may we forsake our idols and pursue our Maker. What does the Scripture say of the one who trusts in God?

> Blessed is the man who trusts in the LORD,
> > whose confidence is in him.
> He will be like a tree planted by the water
> > that sends out its roots by the stream.

It does not fear when heat comes;
>   its leaves are always green.
It has no worries in a year of drought
>   and never fails to bear fruit. (Jer. 17:7–8)

Meditation Moments

1. With which of the following do you struggle: seeing "planks" in others' eyes, envy, idolatry, self-obsession, or fear? In what specific ways do these manifest themselves?
2. Do you struggle in other areas specifically related to single-ness? Consider specific examples.
3. Spend devotional time reading through the book of James in light of these sins and struggles.
4. Have you closed yourself to falling in love? Upon what is this based? How has this played out in specific dating relationships—or the lack of relationships?
5. Could it be that your expectations for a husband have shattered all worthy possibilities? How? What are your expectations and are they realistic? How are they aligned with Scripture (or not)?

4 Rainbow through the Rain: *What We Do with Suffering*

● ● ● ● ● ● ● ● ● ● ● ● ● ● ● ●

Amazing Grace

Perhaps you have been angered by your circumstances or you feel alone. Does God care about your singleness and loneliness? Ponder the vignette "The Long Silence," quoted by John Stott:

> At the end of time, billions of people were scattered on a great plain before God's throne. Most shrank back from the brilliant light before them. But some groups near the front talked heatedly—not with cringing shame, but with belligerence. "Can God judge us? How can he know about suffering?" snapped a pert young brunette. She ripped open a sleeve to reveal a tattooed number from a Nazi concentration camp. "We endured terror . . . beatings . . . torture . . . and death!"

In another group a [black] boy lowered his collar. "What about this?" he demanded, showing an ugly rope burn. "Lynched . . . for no crime but being black!" In another crowd, a pregnant schoolgirl with sullen eyes. "Why should I suffer," she murmured. "It wasn't my fault." Far out across the plain there were hundreds of such groups. Each had a complaint against God for the evil and suffering he permitted in this world. How lucky God was to live in heaven where all was sweetness and light, where there was no weeping or fear, no hunger or hatred. What did God know of all that man had been forced to endure in this world? For God leads a pretty sheltered life, they said.

So, each of these groups sent forth their leader, chosen because he had suffered the most—a Jew, a [black], a person from Hiroshima, a horribly deformed arthritic, a thalidomide child. In the center of the plain they consulted with each other. At last they were ready to present their case. It was rather clever. Before God could be qualified to be their judge, he must endure what they had endured. Their decision was that God should be sentenced to live on earth—as a man!

"Let him be born a Jew. Let the legitimacy of his birth be doubted. Give him a work so difficult that even his family will think he is out of his mind when he tries to do it. Let him be betrayed by his closest friends. Let him face false charges, be tried by a prejudiced jury and convicted by a cowardly judge. Let him be tortured. At the last, let him see what it means to be terribly alone. Then let him die. Let him die so that there can be no doubt that he died. Let there be a great host of witnesses to verify it."

As each leader announced his portion of the sentence, loud murmurs of approval went up from the throng of people assembled. And when the last had finished pronouncing sentence, there was a long silence. No one uttered another word.

No one moved. For suddenly all knew that God had already served his sentence.[1]

Perhaps our cry would be, "Let him never marry; let him live often alone in this world, with few friends—if any—to stand by him through the worst." Even in these, Christ has served the sentence.

Into all these lives, God's mercy shines through. Complete separation from God is found only in hell. Every human still experiences the warmth of the sun and the signs of life as the seasons change. God has not left us. The perfect Substitute, Jesus Christ, experienced the *full* wrath of God and *complete* separation on behalf of his children. This is amazing love, and this is ultimate suffering. When we are frustrated by our own suffering in the world, we must not forget the life of Christ on this earth: "He was pierced for [literally: because of] our transgressions, he was crushed for [because of] our iniquities; the punishment that brought us peace was upon him, and by his wounds we are healed" (Isa. 53:5). The worst things happened to the Best of individuals so that good might result for us. He suffered that we might have life. Why, then, should we be exempt from suffering?

Momentary Troubles

One of my friends proposed several years ago that singleness is suffering. At what age, then, would singleness become suffering? At twenty-five? Thirty-two? Forty-five? And why are we content in our singleness during some stages, while distressed at other moments? We have placed societal expectations and timelines on this subject. Additionally, our current mood or life circumstance

1. Author unknown, quoted in John Stott, *The Cross of Christ* (Downers Grove, IL: InterVarsity Press, 2006), 327–28.

factors heavily into our perception of our single state. Therefore, how can singleness in and of itself be suffering?

Yet singleness does include struggles—as does every other stage of life. Married couples experience loss and disappointment, children have their own experience with suffering, and the elderly must endure deteriorating bodies and impending death. I fear that we single people unintentionally label ourselves as victims when we wallow in our suffering that is due, we believe, to being single. Many live as though life will improve drastically if we marry. Seldom do we expect this other life stage to bring a whole new set of problems and struggles. If we think marriage will rescue us, we are missing the point. We have already been rescued! Christ is the Rescuer.

Instead of seeing singleness as suffering, remember that life as a whole is tainted by the fall. Our sin has ushered in imperfection and broken relationships at every point. The cure for suffering and sin is Jesus Christ. So run quickly to him. In him is full acceptance and forgiveness. I wish I could say that suffering will be taken away as a result, but Scripture makes no such promise. We must look beyond the struggles to the One who suffered so that we might have life and have it to the full. We will not rest fully content and problem-free until the Lord returns. Lord, come quickly!

After much pain and many questions posed to God, Job concluded in the book dedicated to his story:

> I know you can do all things;
>   no plan of yours can be thwarted.
> You asked, "Who is this that obscures my counsel
>   without knowledge?"
>   Surely I spoke of things I did not understand,
>   things too wonderful for me to know. (Job 42:2–3)

God had not given Job a reason for his suffering, but this man was convinced that God is sovereign—period. That knowledge was enough for him. We, too, can be assured, regardless of the circumstances in our lives, that "nothing, therefore, happens unless the Omnipotent wills it to happen. He either allows it to happen, or he actually causes it to happen."[2]

Do you believe this? Does your life reflect this knowledge?

Therefore we do not lose heart. Though outwardly we are wasting away, yet inwardly we are being renewed day by day. For our light and momentary troubles are achieving for us an eternal glory that far outweighs them all. So we fix our eyes not on what is seen, but on what is unseen. For what is seen is temporary, but what is unseen is eternal. (2 Cor. 4:16–18)

Rest from Your Worries

Recently I experienced a week of intense confusion regarding a relationship. Thoughts seemed to swirl around inside my head without much cohesion and sense. I could not resolve the process and outcome, and the stress at one point literally brought an ache to my stomach.

Then a dear woman mentioned something in passing of the flutter and anxiety of Martha, a friend of Jesus. At that moment I realized that our minds can be "worried and upset about many things" (Luke 10:41) and "distracted by all the preparations" before us (v. 40). For years I had interpreted Martha's actions as referring only to physical busyness—which most certainly is a trap for many of us. But even though these verses highlight a specific, physical event, the truths can still be applied to any area of life that overwhelms and draws us

2. St. Augustine, *Enchiridion: On Faith, Hope, and Love,* trans. Albert C. Outler (Dallas, Perkins School of Theology, 1955), chapter 24, http://www.tertullian.org/fathers/augustine_enchiridion_02_trans.htm.

away from the peace that our Savior offers. Martha's sister, Mary, found rest in the Lord by sitting at his feet and listening to him speak (v. 39). Do you remember Christ's response to busyness and confusion—even of the mind? "Only one thing is needed. Mary has chosen what is better, and it will not be taken away from her" (v. 42).

However intangible it may seem, envision sitting at the Lord's feet, laying all your burdens, anxious thoughts, and concerns there, knowing he cares for you. Listen to his words: I am God; I am the Alpha and Omega, the Beginning and the End; I am the Good Shepherd who cares for his sheep; I suffered all anguish and rejection so that you might have life. Remember his character and his promises to you, and of course, go to his Word continually. Our own thoughts can heap on more and more confusion in times of great worry; we need solid reminders of the truths of God. Rest in these truths and sit at his feet, for in this place there is great comfort.

"Come on, Mr. Frodo Dear"

As a tangible picture of Christ's work and presence in our lives, he offers us the body, his church. We are commanded to "carry each other's burdens" (Gal. 6:2). I love the poignant picture of this principle in *The Lord of the Rings*, by J. R. R. Tolkien. In the last book, as Frodo is nearing the end of his journey toward destroying the evil ring, which has almost become a deadly weight, his constant friend Sam exclaims, "Come, Mr. Frodo! I can't carry it for you, but I can carry you and it as well. So up you get. Come on, Mr. Frodo dear!"[3]

3. J. R. R. Tolkien, *The Lord of the Rings: The Return of the King* (New York: Houghton Mifflin, 2004), 940.

60

Are we willing to walk the long road to Mordor[4] with our friends? The path is difficult, yes, and it requires that we endure with our friends and suffer along with them. But let us remember the One who endured the ultimate suffering for us and, in turn, follow his example.

If you are the one suffering, allow the body to minister to you. Do not take up false pride and pretend to be making it with little difficulty. Accept the comfort and support with grace and gratitude. We must be willing to share our needs and be vulnerable in order to truly experience the community that God supplies through the church.

The Rainbow through the Rain

In looking at the trials in life, think again of the beautiful picture painted in the sky through a rainbow. I love the significance that Dr. David Calhoun, professor at Covenant Theological Seminary, draws from this display of God: "A storm is the prerequisite for a rainbow."[5] Do we believe this—that storms must enter our lives so that gorgeous rainbows can then appear in our lives?

George Matheson, a brother in Christ from the nineteenth century, penned these words to the beautiful hymn "O Love That Wilt Not Let Me Go":

O Joy that seekest me through pain,
I cannot close my heart to thee;
I trace the rainbow through the rain,
And feel the promise is not vain
That morn shall tearless be.

4. Mordor was the ultimate place of evil in the *Lord of the Rings* series. Frodo had to endure the arduous journey to this awful place in order to destroy the one remaining evil ring.
5. David Calhoun, "Climbing Rainbows," *Covenant Magazine* (October/ November 1996): 4.

From where did these words come? "I was suffering from extreme mental distress, and the hymn was the fruit of pain," Matheson wrote—some say after his marriage proposal was refused by a young woman, possibly because he was blind.[6] Out of intense pain flowed these beautiful words that have served as a source of comfort to generations following after! Do you believe that God is *seeking* you out in the midst of pain? He promises to be with us even through the valley of the shadow of death (Ps. 23:4). Oh, may we not close our hearts to him, but embrace him in the rain and through the storm, holding on to the promise of the rainbow: God will *not* send rain enough to flood our lives to ruination.

A Way through the Desert

At times, instead of a deluge, we may be experiencing what feels like a desert existence. Maybe you are exhausted; nothing can be seen on the horizon but more of the same, and you are spiritually parched. Has God abandoned you? The Israelites struggled with similar doubts and frustrations as they wandered in the desert for forty years. And yet the reality of God's presence was with them during this time:

> Because of your great compassion you did not abandon them in the desert. By day the pillar of cloud did not cease to guide them on their path, nor the pillar of fire by night to shine on the way they were to take. You gave your good Spirit to instruct them. You did not withhold your manna from their mouths, and you gave them water for their thirst. For forty years you sustained them in the desert; they lacked nothing, their clothes did not wear out nor did their feet become swollen. (Neh. 9:19–21)

6. Charles Seymour Robinson. *Annotations Upon Popular Hymns* (Cincinnati: Cranston & Curtis, 1893), 518.

Since the time of the release from captivity in Egypt, the desert has been a significant place and strong image for Jewish people. The word *desert* surely cannot be read in the Torah or other Jewish literature without a palpable reaction and visceral connection to the past. It is mentioned frequently, as in Hosea 2:14–15, where the Lord says:

> I am now going to allure her;
>> I will lead her into the desert
>> and speak tenderly to her. . . .
> There she will sing as in the days of her youth,
>> as in the day she came up out of Egypt.

I am constantly surprised at how the Lord works—so contrary to our own thoughts of what is good or practical. Odd as it may seem, the desert is God's special place for his people. One of the benefits of the desert is rest: "The people who survive the sword will find favor in the desert; I will come to give rest to Israel" (Jer. 31:2). Who of us would willingly go into the desert for renewal and refreshment? Yet the Lord says, "See, I am doing a new thing! Now it springs up; do you not perceive it? I am making a way in the desert and streams in the wasteland" (Isa. 43:19). Notice that God himself makes the way; he walked with the Israelites *in* the desert through the pillar by day and night; the Lord joined Shadrach, Meshach, and Abednego *in* the furnace, a type of desert; Christ spent forty days *in* the desert fasting and then withstood temptation. God must bring us out of exile and into the desert before he brings us to the Promised Land. If he took us directly to the stream, we would miss his sustaining presence in the desert.

Oh, let us not rush to the streams or sunshine, but relish his abiding presence and provision in the wastelands and storms. These may sometimes seem slow in coming, but wait and take heart! The Lord will not abandon his children. The time that seems never-ending to us is merely a drop in the Lord's bucket of eternity and the course of our own lives.

Deeper Than the Pit So Deep

Corrie ten Boom endured many storms during World War II: while hiding in her home and later in the worst of the Nazi concentration camps. In writing of these horrible camps, she noted in her book *The Hiding Place*, "[We] must tell people what we have learned here. We must tell them that there is no pit so deep that he is not deeper still."[7] What faith! After torture, loss of family and friends, and utter suffering that few of us will ever face, these words were still spoken by faith. God used this woman to touch millions of people—*because of her suffering*! When we are suffering, we would do well to remember those who have gone before who have faced tortures and even death.

Consider these words from Lamentations 3:19–27:

> I remember my affliction and my wandering,
>> the bitterness and the gall.
> I well remember them,
>> and my soul is downcast within me.
> Yet this I call to mind
>> and therefore I have hope:
> Because of the LORD's great love we are not consumed,
>> for his compassions never fail.
> They are new every morning;
>> great is your faithfulness.
> I say to myself, "The LORD is my portion;
>> therefore I will wait for him."

7. Corrie ten Boom, *The Hiding Place* (New York: Bantam, 1974), 217.

The LORD is good to those whose hope is in him,
> to the one who seeks him;
it is good to wait quietly
> for the salvation of the LORD.
It is good for a man to bear the yoke
> while he is young.

The Lord is probably so close behind you, so near in this time of trial, that he is not readily visible. He has designed this very path in his mind and intimate thoughts. It is his *best*; any other way would be inadequate and somehow lacking.

Hannah Hurnard, an author and missionary to Palestine, battled stammering and fear. She came to view these afflictions in the following way:

> I gradually came to realize that these two handicaps which had so tormented me were, in reality, two special love gifts from the Lord. They were the two sharp nails which nailed me to him, so that I could never want or dare to go on my own again.[8]

The Result

The author of the Lamentations passage quoted above is honest about the pain, but does not stay in despair. He remembers the Lord's great love, which is still vibrant and effectual for us today. Wait for the Lord and take hope, but also understand that bearing the yoke, or suffering, is "good," as the passage states. Uniquely through suffering, we can experience the intimate healing and molding touch of our heavenly Father. The place of need cultivates the enrichment of our intimacy with God. "We cannot fully understand the concept

8. Hannah Hurnard, *Hinds' Feet on High Places* (Wheaton, IL: Tyndale House Publishers, 1975), 313.

of an intimate Creator, of Immanuel—God with us—until we've felt God beside us during distressing times, and eternal changes are made in the hidden regions of the heart."[9]

A lovely story is told of a beautiful scarf handed down through generations to a woman. One day her pen leaked on the precious heirloom, creating an ugly stain that threatened to ruin the scarf. She bemoaned the great loss to a friend who offered to take the cloth home and returned the next day with a masterfully renewed scarf. It had been restored far beyond its former beauty by using the ink blot as the beginning of a lovely design that enhanced the whole fabric.[10] And so God takes the mess and pain of our lives and creates a stunning masterpiece.

As stated earlier, suffering refines us; it sands down the prideful, independent tendencies in our hearts and points us back to our Maker. Furthermore, and more significantly, suffering is the way of the cross, the way of Christ. If indeed we call ourselves his followers, we must be willing to share in his sufferings. "If anyone would come after me, he must deny himself and take up his cross and follow me" (Matt. 16:24; see also Mark 8:34; Luke 9:23). This is a lifelong journey of daily surrendering ourselves to Christ. The way of the cross is not easy, but the rewards are eternal and the joy available boundless!

Meditation Moments

1. Reflect on the suffering endured by others or yourself. Has the Lord taught lessons through it or shaped and grown

9. Linda Rutzen, "The Winter Wheat," *Focus on the Family Magazine* (November 1999): 7.
10. Thomas Lane Butts, *Illustrations Unlimited*, ed. James S. Hewett (Wheaton, IL: Tyndale House Publishers, 1988), 16–17.

those involved closer into the image of his Son? Maybe the lessons are not yet clear. What emotions are you facing in light of these and other trials?

2. Do you think you have suffered during your singleness? In what ways has this manifested itself? How is the Lord moving you to respond?

3. Review the Scripture in this chapter during your personal times with the Lord. Let him speak into your heart through his Word!

4. Study Isaiah 35. Notice how God transforms the desert (vv. 1–2), God goes to the desert (vv. 3–4), and God redeems his people *in* the desert (vv. 5–10). What does this mean for your life?

5. Meditate on the following thought: God arranges suffering for our good. To say, "I do not want to suffer," is to say to the Lord, "Don't love me."[11]

---

11. Timothy Keller, head pastor of Redeemer Presbyterian Church in New York City. Used by permission.

5 The Dating Game

· · · · · · · · · · · · · · · · ·

FINALLY: a chapter on dating! You have waited to learn how to get more dates or how to date, period. I have discovered a five-step process to ensure that you will be married in two years.

Dream on! Others may try to make such a claim, but I find no foundation in Scripture or life for such a statement. Yet we still live in a society obsessed with dating and the lifestyles and loves of rich and famous couples, so it is a reality that we must face.

From a young age, a girl is told through various sources that her worth is wrapped up in being pursued by a boy. We put so much stock in whether or not a certain someone speaks to us, the number of dates we go on, or whether the man in question has each of the 103 qualities that the man of our dreams must possess. These and other hang-ups put far too much added weight and pressure on the phenomenon called *dating*. I wish we could follow a certain pattern so that everything would work smoothly in relationships, but, honestly, dating is one of the most topsy-turvy experiences that most of us will face. So regardless of whether we are dating or not, what is a proper and healthy perspective?

The How-tos of Dating

Ease Up

If you are not dating, it's okay! It is not the end of the world; all is not lost; you are not alone.

There is far too much concern about not dating. Why? We single women are insecure and desperately desire others to approve of us—especially men. As has been mentioned, everything in our society points toward being accepted and acceptable. Bottom line: when we despair about not dating, we are lacking belief in God's plan for our lives. I can say this boldly because I myself am struggling right now as I write this. Tonight I saw a man who recently asked me out and then totally dropped the ball after one date. The feelings of frustration, doubt, and insecurity immediately came to the surface. At this moment, I am having to make a choice to believe that God is in control of my life instead of to think that he has forgotten and mope that I may be single for life.

Perhaps I will always be single, but I can choose my response. In such instances, we can spiral downward or, in a sense, throw it all back up to God, asking him to take the situation and allow us to live in freedom again. Whether or not we are dating loses its import when we believe that God is working out his plan and has not left us alone.

A Match Made in Heaven

When you see an attractive single man or meet one who intrigues you, what is your gut instinct? Think about it for a moment. Do you try to strike up a conversation or hang on to one as long as possible, regardless of his body language? You might sit in the back left corner of the auditorium because *he* will be sitting in your direct line of vision to the front. You may halfheartedly listen to a friend at a party because your crush has just walked through the door. At the close of the evening, maybe you position yourself near the door as he is leaving—even though your hurting friend needs to talk in the opposite corner.

We women are perfectionists when it comes to manipulation of men. It is all in a day's work. This may sound harsh, but we know how to weasel our way into and out of situations. We will bulldoze over people to get what we want. Of course, this is the tendency of the human heart; unfortunately, it is destructive for us. One of my friends said specifically about romantic interests that "we manipulate to get what we want, only to find out that it's not at all what we want."

I am not advocating isolation from men or frumpy attire. We should be out and about and available. But we must also search our hearts' motivations for our actions. As you interact with men, be yourself; don't try to overimpress. Also, try to keep from shaping a whole evening around a love interest whom you are not even dating. Remember, there are other people to enjoy and know. A lot of time can be wasted on a dead-end street.

We also try to spark an interest or start a romance simply for the sake of the experience. It seems intriguing. "Enamored with the idea of love . . . in love with loving, I was casting about for something to love."[1] This is basically selfish and has little to do with pursuing genuine love.

1. Saint Augustine, *The Confessions*, trans. Maria Boulding (New York: Vintage Books, 1997), 37.

How quickly we cease trusting God to be our matchmaker. He knows our hearts, and he knows the best mate for us. Allow him to order your heart and relationships. This is very hard and requires much prayer for wisdom.

Awakening Love

Song of Songs has long been an intriguing book to many. It certainly lends beauty and passion to romantic love. Obviously, the Lord approves of romance and gives us the opportunity for this pleasure.

Yet we cannot escape this repeated phrase in the book: "Do not arouse or awaken love until it so desires" (Song 2:7, 3:5, 8:4). The fact that it appears three times must be for good reason. I believe this short statement is a warning to hold back until love is ripe and ready. Do not give your heart freely and frivolously. May the Lord give us wisdom to know!

But there is also a beautiful delight in this exhortation: when it desires, love is right and can be wonderful. God has a time for everything, even "a time to embrace and a time to refrain" (Eccl. 3:5).

The Bottom Line

In the midst of the Dating Game (for it so often feels like a game!), remember to step back and not take it too seriously—at least at first. If and when dating comes along, just enjoy getting to know someone better. Appreciate the man as a fellow creature—a creation of the heavenly God. I am ashamed to admit that my past is littered with men whom I did not treat with dignity. I shunned several of them because of my own insecurities and because I was too concerned that they might like me even more if I were nice. But even if we refuse a man, it should be with grace and politeness. If a man asks you out on a date, he is putting himself on the line. Often, apparently, asking for a date is no small feat for a man; it can require a lot of courage.

Whether or not you always say yes to a first date is up to your own discretion. One word of caution, however: we can be very hasty in our assessments of men. For some of them, if we would give them a chance, our perception might alter. On the other hand, if you are asked by someone you legitimately do not want to date and you do not have plans on the specific night, do not say that you do. Do not make excuses or, worse, lie. A simple "no, thank you, I'm not interested" will suffice. This might sound cruel, but honesty is one of the highest priorities in dating. Honesty is also crucial anytime after the first date when you are no longer interested. Do not drag a man further along into a relationship that you don't want to be in; his heart is involved and not something with which to trifle. Cut it off when you sense that it is time.

Remember that every dating relationship has struggles. It is vital to stay in communication with the Lord for his direction. Also, you must have wise counsel to help you navigate through the emotions. I find that my vision is most clouded in the throes of a romance. Don't trust your own heart, but confide in one you trust.

Consumer Shopping

"The man of your dreams is available and for sale on videocassette."[2] This was the guarantee at the beginning of the video before I watched *Roman Holiday* one evening. Hollywood has bent over backward to make idealistic romance seem readily available. Unfortunately, this mentality has crept into the dating scene. We think that the special and perfect man

2. *Roman Holiday*, directed by William Wyler (Paramount Pictures, 1953).

of our dreams is out there—possibly even just around the corner—and available for purchase. Maybe one good-looking person comes along, so we try him out, only to see someone who might be more appealing a few weeks later. The first one is ditched; our hopes are elevated again. Oh, but then there just may be an even better option . . . .

First of all, this practice breeds discontent. We want perfection and will not accept flaws in another. We live in a world of the latest and greatest technology. There is always a new software package. In the computer age, we have moved from desktop to laptop to Palm to BlackBerry within the span of a few years. I can hardly keep up with the names, much less the technology.

Not only are we looking for the best buy and highest quality, we are trying to package ourselves perfectly, too. Don't forget to hide that blemish or wear the right lipstick color. Dating really has become a game. We are constantly trying to outdo the next woman—either with ourselves or with the man on our arm.

Get Off the Sidetrack!

We too often become sidetracked by our daydreams about specific men. Possibly you long to date a certain man and feel an intense attraction toward him. Healthy attraction is a positive feeling or reaction toward a man who is effectively pursuing you, but can be painful if directed at a long shot. I am ashamed to admit that I was infatuated with the same guy for the better part of seven years! He had shown brief inklings of possible interest in me, but we had never even been on an official date. That experience showed me the strong pull of desire and its impact on our lives. I spent much time in prayer over that individual, asking God to take away my feelings for him. But the question is, what replaced those thoughts?

After thinking back on that infatuation and attraction toward men in general, I have become more and more aware of the futility of such thoughts outside of a dating relationship. First of all, our mental energies are taken up with thoughts about another with whom we are not even romantically involved. I am convinced that the Lord has better uses for our thought life.

A good check against uncontrolled thoughts about men and the scheming to which those desires can lead is remembering that those men (except one, if God has a husband picked out) are intended for another. This has been a very sobering thought for me. Barring the horrible pain of widowhood or divorce, I believe God has each man for one woman only. Wait patiently for the man God has chosen for you, and pray fervently for perseverance to live before all others as a godly, encouraging sister in Christ.

As a side note, quite frankly, if a man is not pursuing you, he is not really interested. If he were, he would pursue. It seems that once a man has a plan, intention, or attraction, he acts.

E-Harmony

I am not hearing a harmonious symphony in the background as I try to tackle the debate about the benefits and curses of Internet dating. Most of us probably know couples who have met and married through the Internet. I personally have a friend who met her wonderful, godly husband online, and they now have a beautiful daughter. I was thrilled to watch them through their courtship, was honored to be a part of their wedding, and believe God brought these two together.

Yet I feel that I must highlight some of the negatives of this option, for it is not a harmonious experience for *all* those who subscribe. One of my friends likened Internet dating to a drug: once she tried it, she was hooked and couldn't stay off the computer for long in the endless hope of finding "the one." She went through man after man, only to end up disappointed and dateless for another weekend. If by chance she did "meet" someone online who wanted to get together in person, the reality was often a letdown. Finally, after sheer exhaustion and frustration, she quit.

Also, this venue seems to offer an ongoing ability to look for the perfect person. You are able to list exactly what you want in a mate. Do any of us really know anyway, and could we meet the requirements in our own list? I have concluded that I actually have no idea who would be best for me, and I look forward to finding out when and if God brings my husband. Far be it from me to have to put together a qualifying checklist that he would have to pass.

One last thought on this subject: if God can bring two people together through a computer, he can certainly use any other circumstance to make it happen. He moves mountains. I always say that I could meet my husband tripping down the stairs of some random building in a foreign city. Yes, God can use a computer, but he is so far above and beyond the confines of a piece of machinery.

What Has Gone Wrong with Relationships?

I believe Satan has woven a web of deceit around the topic of dating outside *and* inside the church. We as women are encouraged to be self-sufficient and independent—valuable traits, to a degree, in our society. But when we take these characteristics into our relationships with others—and, more importantly, God—they can be detrimental.

Many men are now unsure of how to act around women. Recently, my father was even treated with disdain by a woman when he tried to hold a door open for her. This effort used to be a sign of respect toward women; we have now turned it into an offense! Why should we not be flattered by a man offering us his seat or allowing us to walk through a door first? Not only have we taken away a piece of our own dignity, we have stripped the man of his, too. I believe that the male sex is affirmed by serving us in these ways. Allow men to be men! God has made them caretakers and providers, roles they perform well when allowed. In dancing, the most joy and freedom for me come when I step out of my desire to lead and let the man guide me. Only then can great beauty and grace be displayed and, ironically, both partners end up looking strong. It takes two to tango—but one must lead.

I hear countless complaints that men don't ask women out. But is it only their fault? If you want to encourage men to ask women out, start by affirming masculinity. Be flattered if a male friend walks on the street side of a sidewalk; perhaps even thank him. Men have lost all sense of manhood: many cannot even treat a woman to a meal anymore, for example.

Also, ask yourself whether you are continuing to hold up the romantic ideal. Is he good-looking enough? Does he make enough money? How does he dress? Let me ask all of us to consider by whose standards we are rating the potential interest. Often not by the standards of the Lord, who does not look at the outward appearance but at the heart. Some wise advice I received from my brother-in-law regarding a recent relationship was to pray that God would show me the man's heart. This is, in the long run, what matters most. We should approach all friendships from this perspective: looking at the inside instead of the outside. Such depth and richness can be found in this pursuit.

The Real Thing

During one season of my single adult life, all of a sudden I found myself with several possibilities on the horizon. Granted, these were not all considered official dates, but they were new men to meet. The sources were quite varied and some even humorous. (Think of a blind date with your aunt's brother's former boss's nephew's cousin.) I assure you that I had never experienced such a waterfall of single men I had never met before.

One man, whom I had briefly met and seen only a few times, contacted me out of the blue and arranged a meeting, to me an encouraging and bold gesture on his part. So my curiosity and even my hope were ignited. I was amazed to see how quickly I became interested to meet and get to know this person. Perhaps he would be "the one." And just maybe he would be kind and take initiative and follow through, qualities I appreciate.

In the end, however, the date did not turn out as I had expected, for many reasons and several surprise changes. It reminded me that we are constantly looking for perfection and we long to be pursued consistently and lovingly. It was as if God whispered in my ear that these qualities can be found completely only in Christ. If we seek them solely in a man, we will be disappointed—as a man would be in us. Also, it is an insane amount of pressure to put on the man, much less yourself and the evening. We can hope to find reflections of wonderful qualities in others, but they will be imperfect. Christ himself is the real "image of the invisible God" (Col. 1:15). Recognizing this will allow us to enjoy life more fully and accept the flaws without the pressure of perfection looming over all our relationships. And I believe it will make us more thankful when we see God changing and, yes, perfecting lives.

Meditation Moments

1. What is the perception about dating among your peers? Your family? Do you feel pressures to date?
2. What are your greatest struggles about dating?
3. How do you feel when you are not dating? What insecurities does this bring up?
4. Are you a consumer shopper when it comes to men and dating?
5. Are you ever sidetracked by thoughts of men, or do you struggle with the thought that you may never marry? How can these thoughts be approached?
6. In what ways can you more actively seek to affirm men in their masculinity?
7. How do you think God would have you view dating? How can the picture of Christ in Colossians 1:15–20 transform your perception?

6   The Object of
Our Affection

First Things First

Who and what are the top people and priorities in your life? (Our actions and time investments can certainly provide a strong clue.) Much of life is spent in finding out the answer and continually reprioritizing. C. S. Lewis, a great Christian thinker of the mid-twentieth century, stated:

> You can't get second things by putting them first; you can get second things only by putting first things first. From which it would follow that the question, What things are first? is of concern not only to philosophers but to everyone.[1]

This statement causes us to grapple with the often-stated relational dimension of Christianity, as I did recently in my own journal:

1. C. S. Lewis, *Time and Tide*, reprinted in *God in the Dock* (Grand Rapids: Eerdmans, 1970), 280.

I have a hard time grasping the intimacy aspect of Christianity. Of course, I know it's a relationship, but what does that REALLY mean? *Lord* (of the universe, no less!), *what do you say? How do you view our time together?* I know you died for me, that I am one for whom you wrote your "love letter," and that you discern my going out and coming in. But why? Why would you want a relationship with me? What does this truly mean? It seems that I find it easier believing you are God and sovereign over my life than understanding intimacy with you. I know you did come down as a man, God incarnate—and that you indwell us now through the power of the Holy Spirit and *will* dwell among us after our time on earth is done. Is that the point: that we can—but not yet fully—know this intimacy with God?

Perhaps the reality is that I will catch only a glimpse here on earth. Herein is perhaps a fresh perspective for me on 1 Corinthians 13! "Love never fails"—from the garden, through humanity and the cross until the end of time and the dawning of eternity. Prophecies, tongues, and [incomplete] knowledge will pass away. NOW I see but a poor reflection of love, intimacy, and relationship; I know only in part. THEN I shall see God face to face, which will be true intimacy!

However hard to understand while we are here on earth, God does desire intimacy with us. This relationship must be first because it will inform all others. Are you desiring and seeking intimacy with a man? Begin first with the Lord. Only when we seek to be right with God can we begin to be truly right with others. This is a lifelong discovery—one that we must pursue now and throughout the entirety of our lives.

Jesus Loves . . . and So Much More

"Jesus loves me! This I know, for the Bible tells me so."

A wonderful place to start this journey with God is in the lyrics of this seemingly simplistic song. But contemplate the *layers* of truth beneath it! God's love created us in his image: each unique, yet each one reflecting qualities of the Creator. His love redeemed and called a people unto himself. His unfailing passion pursued this broken, faithless people—even throughout generations. The ultimate expression of his love was sending his Son to the cross to die for sinners, "that we should be called children of God" (1 John 3:1).

God is the only One who is completely loving without fault. Not only this, but he is merciful, just, gracious, compassionate, slow to anger, holy, patient, and powerful, to name just a few of his other attributes.

If all this is true *and* we believe it, thanksgiving flows forth and our perception of our lives will be transformed.

> Gratitude is important because it has the power to change our attitude. When we are willing to give thanks to God in *all* things, not just some things—to consciously thank him even when we don't feel very grateful—something in us begins to shift. We begin to see life as Christ sees it, full of opportunities rather than obstacles. And when we view life through eyes of faith, fear just has to flee.[2]

We as believers must have faith in God's love and his truth. We are inclined to hope too fervently to see consistent love and truth in mankind. Instead, we must hope most fervently in the Lord! To what does our anxiety and worry about singleness lead? More anxiety and worry. It profits nothing, but makes our hearts sick and weary. It clouds our vision so that we cannot clearly see the Lord.

2. Joanna Weaver, *Having a Mary Heart in a Martha World* (Colorado Springs: WaterBrook Press, 2004), 41.

Has not the Lord ordained that I now be single? If it were wrong or out of his plan, I would be declaring that he is not God. As single women, we are being coerced into dividing our hearts by desiring what God has not yet placed before or opened to us.

Do you long for contentment in the present? Believe in God and his character.

The Truth

Do you believe that God desires a relationship with you? What is the extent of his love? If we go back to the garden of Eden, we will realize that the reason God created us was for relationship with him. Adam and Eve could actually *hear* the Lord himself "walking in the garden in the cool of the day" (Gen. 3:8). Can you imagine this? A precious friend of mine recently shared with me the joy she has in knowing that there are memories that only she and the Lord share. The two of them remember many long walks together, discovering beauties that no one else has experienced with her. Can you picture yourself going on a walk with God? This may sound ludicrous to you, but why not try to envision it? Ask him to go along with you the next time you walk. He is with you anyway—not physically, but you can still talk with him and praise him for the surrounding creation.

The words of Psalm 139 are deeply intimate, specifically verses 1–4:

> O LORD, you have searched me
>   and you know me.
> You know when I sit and when I rise;
>   you perceive my thoughts from afar.
> You discern my going out and my lying down;
>   you are familiar with all my ways.

84

Before a word is on my tongue
    you know it completely, O LORD.

These verses are meant to be completely comforting and nonjudgmental. I am sure that none of us have completely pure thoughts and words, for which we need the grace and forgiveness of God—but no condemnation is heard in the psalmist's words. God loves us not because of anything we have done. He *wants* to know us; he wants to hear our thoughts. For those of us who had loving parents, we know that they were interested when we told them about the tents we built with our best friends or when we put on a great play for them and dressed up in Mom's old prom dresses. In the same way, our heavenly Father wants to hear about the townhouse we would like to purchase or the presentation we have to make at work.

Recall the words of the Prince to Snow White, quoted at the beginning of this book: "I love you more dearly than anything else in the world. Come with me to my father's castle, and be my wife."[3] This is the truth we have in Christ! "I have redeemed you; I have called you by name; you are mine" (Isa. 43:1). He calls to *you*; he loves *you* with an everlasting love. He awakens his own from death, because we sinned by eating the apple, and he bids us come to his Father's palace. This earth is merely a preparation, a dim shadow of what is to come. The ultimate fulfillment of our longings is Christ, the true Object of our affection. He has gone to prepare a far better home for us. The story of redemption is the *true* fairy tale! Even the most wonderful husband will never fill our deepest longings and will fail us, as we will fail him. Not so with our heavenly Bridegroom. May we fill our lives and hearts with thoughts of him. May

3. *Classic Fairy Tales* (Seymour, CT: Greenwich Workshop Press, 2003), 60.

the truths of his character and his calling to us disintegrate all doubts.

The Path of True Love

Mawage! Mawage is wot bwings us togeder tooday. Mawage, that bwessed awangement, that dweam within a dweam . . . then wuv, twoo wuv will fowwow you forevah . . . so treasure your wuv.[4]

Most of us can name that movie without a pause. But these expressions by the clergyman in *The Princess Bride* were anything but true about Buttercup and Prince Humperdinck. Yet the sentiments describe a longing we all have: we dream of true love; we seek it in earthly relationships.

Recently my mother and I were discussing the seeming rise in the number of single people. To add a lighthearted comment to the moment, I declared, "Tonight at church I am going to meet the love of my life." I had actually experienced years of hoping that very thing whenever I went to church or a party. Now it seems an opportunity instead to smile, give it up to God, and marvel at how and when he might actually bring the meeting to pass.

Little did I know when speaking those words that, in fact, they were true. As I stood in church singing to the Lord, I realized that I *had* met the love of my life: Christ is the love that will remain throughout my life and take me into eternity. It was such a special realization.

A relationship with God mirrors several aspects of earthly relationships quite well. This is because God, a relational being, has created us in his image. As we all know, relationships take time, care, and attention. Do we really expect to develop a close-

4. *The Princess Bride*, directed by Rob Reiner (MGM/UA Studios, 1987).

ness with a friend if we do not call her, spend time with her, or remember to ask her about her concerns? So it is with our heavenly Father. We cannot expect to get to know him deeply if we merely show up at church once a week and say a quick prayer when we have a need. Although he is God, think about him for a moment as a person—as a human friend. Would you expect intimacy with him if you treated him as casually as described above? He does not give up on us or disappear for a few days, so that makes us responsible for any lack of relationship. Therefore, where do we begin to grow in our love relationship with God? We can better acquaint ourselves with our Lord in several ways. Let's explore a few.

Time

So much time is spent longing after our future husbands, but how about the time invested longing after our heavenly Bridegroom? Are we so enamored of our Lord that we love to sit at his feet in the posture of Mary, affirmed by Jesus? "You are worried and upset about many things, but only one thing is needed. Mary has chosen what is better, and it will not be taken away from her" (Luke 10:41–42). May we cease our proclivity to rush around and be worried and upset about a myriad of things.

Recently my family was all together for Thanksgiving. We had the meals to prepare, projects with the kids to complete, things to show each other; the list could go on. Before long, we were all stressed and frustrated with each other and found the to-do list impeding the fellowship that we had come to enjoy! So it is many times with God. The busyness of our lives too often shuts out the Lord. This world continually woos us away, and we find that we have forgotten our first love.

Obviously, we cannot spend every moment without activity, sitting only at Jesus' feet. But we must devote some time to this heart posture: still before God, ready to hear from him. And the whole of our lives should be lived before God. As you go through your daily activities, go with God, sensing his presence with you, inviting him to be with you and guide you, praying for his presence and wisdom throughout the day.

Consider this scenario: At 6 A.M., the clock radio wakes you up. Of course, you want to catch the news, so you keep it on while you wake up a little. After a workout at the gym with an instructor or in front of a TV, you turn the radio on when you get into the bathroom. Don't forget about catching a bit of some talk show while you are eating breakfast. Since you are running late, you listen to praise music on the way to work to try to focus on God. Sound familiar? I am convinced that Satan has used media and entertainment to pull us from *quiet* time with God. Of course, it is not all negative, but we need to monitor what and how much is going into our minds and hearts through our eyes and ears. Spend time in silence. Try *not* turning on the radio the minute you get into your car, or decide that you will not watch TV for a certain amount of time. We must be intentional about setting aside time with our Lord.

Scripture Study

Do we long to know our Lord intimately? "Meditate on [the Word] day and night," as God urged Joshua (Josh. 1:8). Joshua had a nation to lead, a new job to learn, and a country to conquer; he was quite a busy man! But time in the Word was to bookend his day; Scripture was to permeate his thoughts.

Maybe you do not sense that God is at work; you feel that he is far away. After years of no dates, one of my friends often laments, "I wish God would just show up." But Scripture tells us that God *has* shown up—through Christ. "As God has said: 'I will live with them and walk among them, and

I will be their God, and they will be my people'" (2 Cor. 6:16, quoting Lev. 26:12). God's passion for us sent his Son to this earth as a baby and carried him to the cross so that now God might dwell within us! Christ cried out on the cross and heard no response from the Father so that we might have open communication with our Maker. Do you sense the intimacy of these actions from the Lord? He desires a deep relationship with *us*!

We see Christ most clearly in his Word. John 1 speaks of Christ as the Word that dwelt among us. This Word was in the beginning; it was with God, and was God. The Word created all things; in him was life, the light of men. And then this Word became *flesh* and dwelt among us! This to me is an extremely intimate account—as well as a complex one, requiring study and exploration. First of all, the Lord of the universe allowed himself to be an embryo contained within a human uterus. Then he lived in a family under sinful parents and with selfish siblings. Finally, he lived in close relationship with twelve fallen men, three very intimately.

Do we seek Christ in his Word—the book of wisdom? Proverbs 8:35 says of wisdom, "For whoever finds me finds life and receives favor from the LORD." Is not life what we truly desire—abundant, full, and joyful? Such life is what God offers us through the path of wisdom and his Word. Our Father desires a deep, intimate relationship with you! I believe many single women beg God for a mate while their love relationship with their Maker is stale. He wants our hearts and our service for his kingdom. "Seek first his kingdom"—found most readily in his Word—"and all these things will be given to you as well" (Matt. 6:33).

Maybe you have never really spent much time on your own reading the Bible. It can seem rather daunting. How should you begin? Most importantly, whenever you approach his Word, pray for God to teach you and open the truths it contains. In choosing what to read, you may want to start with a broad overview by reading through the Bible in its entirety. Or you could start with a New Testament book—perhaps one of the first four that detail Christ's life and ministry: Matthew, Mark, Luke, or John. Some people enjoy reading a psalm a day. Recently, I have taken time to review the previous Sunday's sermon, using it as a springboard for further study. Regardless of your preference, remember that the Bible is God's Word and that he wants you to know him through it. Continually look for ways in which you can apply Scripture to your life; ask questions of it; refer to other sections to seek answers. Approach it as an interactive study. Don't read passively, but *look to be changed.*

As an example of the richness of God's Word, let us study more closely several verses of Psalm 25.

Show me your ways, O LORD, teach me your paths. (v. 4)

Do we truly desire for—and ask—God to show us his ways, as this verse models? This involves recognition that God's ways are best. It shows a life of complete trust in God. Then we simply ask him to show us his ways and teach us his paths. Search the Scriptures for evidences of those ways and paths. This one verse might lead to a study on the life of Jesus, discovering how he lived on this earth. What were his ways, and which paths did he take?

He guides the humble in what is right and teaches them his way. (v. 9)

Do you want God's guidance? This verse directs us to humility, which is displayed when we recognize the futility of our own ways. I fear that we tend to be more like the strong-willed child in the throes of a temper tantrum. Before we can be taught, we must be humble and willing. Ask God to show you how you are not humble. There is a promise, then, that he will teach us his ways.

> All the ways of the LORD are loving and faithful for those who keep the demands of his covenant. (v. 10)

Do we truly believe that all his ways are loving and faithful? If so, *none* of life's circumstances are mistakes; nothing God withholds is because he is unloving or unfair; but *all* these circumstances are to express his ultimate love and faithfulness. This verse leads us to the cross because we cannot keep the demands of his covenant, which are complete faithfulness to him and obedience in following his laws. We cannot, but *he* can—and did—on the cross. To this we cling, and in this we have hope for his loving and faithful ways.

Scripture Memory

> I have hidden your word in my heart
>   that I might not sin against you. (Ps. 119:11)

Ask how much of life is fraught with worry and wondering. And yet God's Word speaks into life: "For the word of God is living and active. Sharper than any double-edged sword, it penetrates even to dividing soul and spirit, joints and marrow; it judges the thoughts and attitudes of the heart" (Heb. 4:12).

A friend of mine recently shared the trouble she had been having with sleeping. So she has memorized Psalm 4:8: "I will lie down and sleep in peace, for you alone, O LORD, make me dwell in safety." Nightly she recalls this verse and is greatly comforted. As my friend did, we, too, should memorize Scripture so that we can call on it in times of need. Christ himself had committed words of Scripture to memory. He spoke the words of Psalm 31:5 on the cross: "Into your hands I commit my spirit." He also used Scripture three times to combat the attacks of Satan. If the perfect Lord Jesus as a human learned Scripture, how much more should I!

Start small. Hunt for a passage that speaks directly to a circumstance you are facing. To aid in memorizing, some people prefer the text written on index cards. You can carry the verses with you or recite them aloud each morning or evening. Stick them to your mirror or take them with you to review as you commute to work. Or keeping a journal might be more helpful for you.

I will admit that Scripture memorization is an area of great neglect in my life—much to my detriment! God has given us his Word to help, uphold, comfort, and encourage us. It has the power to change lives. So let us embrace it and absorb it into our beings.

Prayer

Just as you must communicate in a friendship, you must be in dialogue—or prayer—with God. Theologian John Stott recently spoke at a meeting I attended, focusing on the amazing truth in Ephesians 2:18 that we "have access" to God, which is essentially prayer. This ability to talk to the Father is through the Son and by the Spirit—a unique and mysterious Trinitarian experience. It is a phenomenal reality of the Christian life.

God has called us to "pray continually" (1 Thess. 5:17) and promises to be near us when we pray (Deut. 4:7). You might take up prayer-walking, which can be done alone or with a friend. Walk in your neighborhood or near your workplace, praying for people you pass, businesses, family homes, and so on. This can be a powerful tool for joining with God in his missional approach toward your community or city.

One of the most difficult aspects of prayer for me is *focus.* My mind wanders incessantly or I find myself lulled into a sleeplike state—not an ideal recipe for a vibrant prayer life! Therefore, I have recently begun writing out my prayers—not all the words, but just enough to capture the gist. This has done wonders for my concentration; it keeps me on task. For those of you who are as neurotic as I am about not wasting paper, use scraps from anywhere that can be thrown away. This is merely a suggested tool. However they are prayed, God will definitely remember your sincere prayers.

Scripture is filled with prayers of those who have gone before us—Abraham, Moses, and David, to name a few. People in biblical times were called to pray for the peace of Jerusalem (Ps. 122:6), for those who persecuted them (Matt. 5:44), for strength to resist temptation (Luke 22:40), for continued spiritual growth (Eph. 1:17–19a), and in times of trouble (James 5:13). We can use these supplications as guides and even borrow their language.

In Abraham's life, the foundations for his prayers and belief were the covenant[5] promises of God, his character, and his covenant relationship with Abraham. Some of God's promises to Abraham were not fulfilled for hundreds of years! We are given license to plead with God based on who he is and what he promises. Are our prayers just a list of desires, or are they based on God's promises and his character, as well as his covenantal relationship with us? Praying from a foundation of the truths of God and our relationship with him can radically change our prayers.

5. In ancient times, a covenant was a legally binding agreement between two parties. An animal was slaughtered and cut, followed by the ceremonial passing of the two parties between the sacrificed pieces. This act signified that if the covenant were broken by one, his own life could then be taken.

God has entered into a covenant with us. Because we have broken the covenant, our lives are required. But God, through Jesus' death, has paid the price that we owe! For a beautiful illustration of a merciful and glorious covenant that God Almighty makes with Abraham, read Genesis 15.

Prayer is a mysterious exhortation to the Christian, not one that is easily explained. But this I know: I am to pray, for the Bible tells me so! God is completely sovereign, but my prayers still make a difference. They definitely change me; they place me humbly at the feet of my Lord. Also, they allow me to open my eyes and expect the Lord to work. Of course, his working is often different from my expectations—but his way is better in the long run. Furthermore, the Lord of the universe miraculously and mysteriously allows me to participate in his kingdom work through prayer. Don't wait to understand prayer; just get busy doing it, expectant for God to be working.

Praying the Word

Maybe you are used to praying to God, but a unique approach might be to speak back his own Word to him in prayer. (This, of course, comes more easily if we have hidden some of it in our hearts!) A good place to start is with the prayer of a father in Mark 9:24: "I do believe; help me overcome my unbelief!"

God has promised much in his Word. If we are having trouble believing, we can bring the truths of his Word to him in prayer, such as those in Psalm 145:13–17:

> Your kingdom is an everlasting kingdom,
>   and your dominion endures through all
>   generations.
>
> The LORD is faithful to all his promises
>   and loving toward all he has made.
> The LORD upholds all those who fall
>   and lifts up all who are bowed down.
> The eyes of all look to you,
>   and you give them their food at the proper time.

94

You open your hand
    and satisfy the desires of every living thing.

The LORD is righteous in all his ways
    and loving toward all he has made.

He has not promised me a husband, but he has promised to:

Uphold those who fall. Yes, a fall might happen, but God is the Great Rescuer ("God will help her at break of day"—Ps. 46:5). When you falter, pray, "Lord, uphold me!"

Give food at the proper time. He provides at the proper time for us, as he did for his children, the Israelites, as they wandered in the desert so long ago (Ex. 16–17). Again we must choose to believe that his proper time does not follow our own timetable! In times of need, say, "Lord, provide in your proper time and sustain me until then."

Satisfy the desires of every living thing. Conceivably this is the hardest promise to embrace. How do we pray regarding our desires?

Furthermore, what does the Lord say of our desires? "Delight yourself in the LORD and he will give you the desires of your heart" (Ps. 37:4). So if I desire a husband, then he will grant one to me, right? *No!* It is bold, brazen, and presumptuous to think that all our desires are right and best. Remember, his ways are not our ways. They are far above even the good of which we could dream! We are to delight in him, period. As a by-product, he will put in our hearts the desires that are after his heart: godliness, compassion, and humility, for example. If we are first delighting in the Lord, his desires will become our desires. Frankly, we should not even concentrate on the second half of this oft-quoted verse in Psalm 37. Giving you the desires of your heart (or, stated another way, putting godly desires in your heart) is up to God! Our responsibility is to delight in God. Far too often, this verse is used almost as a justification to request exactly what we want. In recent years, I have often thought that if God had given me one particular man I once desired as a husband, I would have been depressed and miserable. Also, the direction my life has taken could not have happened if I were married. God knows best.

You might feel with all earnestness that you are trying to delight in him, but that marriage is still your desire. It may well be that he has put the desire in your heart to be married. But its outworking is to be in his timing. Because he is a good God, the path of our lives is on his timetable. Rest in the goodness of his sovereign timing. Also, be assured that the desire for and institution of marriage is good. Yet our response to this desire could be very questionable—possibly even sinful—and might also become extremely discouraging. To put it candidly, if we are truly walking with God and we are single, then *this* is what he currently has for us! Much regarding our desires must be brought before him in prayer. Search the Scriptures for the prayers of those who have gone before us.

Before you try to find all the singles of the Scriptures, be aware that this will be hard to determine. Interestingly, the marital status of individuals doesn't seem to be of number-one importance to God in his Word. Their identity isn't wrapped up in this categorization, as it sadly often is today. That is not what lasts for eternity; only our standing regarding God's kingdom is of eternal importance. The devotion of the people in the Bible to Jesus is what remains and is proclaimed throughout the ages. May we learn from them!

Some other possible prayers from Scripture are:

- Lord, may your name and renown be the desire of my heart (Isa. 26:8).
- Teach me, Lord, what constitutes your joy ("The joy of the LORD is [my] strength"—Neh. 8:10).
- May "the worries of this life and the deceitfulness of wealth" not choke out your Word (Matt. 13:22).

Praying Scripture is not for the halfhearted because it calls us out of our comfort. "Teach me your *way*, O LORD" (Ps. 86:11) refers to the way of the cross. Do we love and trust God enough to pray these bold prayers that will call us to lives of surrender, love, and mercy? This is the way of the Lord. Will we follow?

Remember, "The LORD is faithful to all his promises and loving toward all he has made" (Ps. 145:13b). I believe he allows us to be bold and come back to him with his promises—and with our difficulty in believing them. You might be struggling to accept that he is loving to you. Reflect on Psalm 77:1–9:

> I cried out to God for help;
> > I cried out to God to hear me.
> When I was in distress, I sought the Lord;
> > at night I stretched out untiring hands
> > and my soul refused to be comforted.
>
> I remembered you, O God, and I groaned;
> > I mused, and my spirit grew faint.
> You kept my eyes from closing;
> > I was too troubled to speak.

97

I thought about the former days,
the years of long ago;
I remembered my songs in the night.
My heart mused and my spirit inquired:

"Will the Lord reject forever?
Will he never show his favor again?
Has his unfailing love vanished forever?
Has his promise failed for all time?
Has God forgotten to be merciful?
Has he in anger withheld his compassion?"

How many of us have prayed a similar prayer? Asaph, the writer of this psalm, was distressed. He asked, "Has his promise failed for all time?" (v. 8). So it felt!

Notice that this open and honest prayer of Asaph was included unedited in God's Word. This proves that we, too, can be honest before the Lord with our aches and disappointments. The key is in remembering the goodness of God and always coming back to him. Asaph did not abandon God. He cried out, sought the Lord, stretched out untiring hands, and remembered God.

So what was his solution?

"To this I will appeal: the years of the right hand of the Most High" (Ps. 77:10). Consider all the past faithfulness of the Lord. Pastor Glenn Hoburg wrote, "If you cannot base your confidence upon his history of faithfulness, you may find yourself shutting down in despair or bitterness."[6] Remember what the Lord has done and do not despair. Start a list if you need to be visually reminded of his works on your behalf. The first truth can be that he has redeemed you and called you by name; you are *his*. Great

6. Glenn Hoburg, "The Waiting Room," *Covenant Magazine* (August/September 1997): 8–10.

is his faithfulness! May this be our conclusion—whatever our life circumstance.

I Want to Know Christ

Do you want to know Christ? I assume so, since you have read this far. Think a moment about what this statement means to you: "I want to know Christ."

It may mean growing in the areas covered in this chapter. Those are all outpourings of a walk with God, of course. But what was Paul's assessment of knowing Christ? "I want to know Christ and the power of his resurrection and the fellowship of sharing in his sufferings, becoming like him in his death, and so, somehow, to attain to the resurrection from the dead" (Phil. 3:10–11). Reread this passage slowly and try to grasp its implications!

These verses are not for the fair-weather Christian. When I first truly meditated on this sentence, I was, quite honestly, terrified. The ramifications were too huge for me to accept. I still tremble when I carefully contemplate them.

These declarations of Paul call us to a life of radical pursuit of Christ. They push us out of our comfort-seeking mentalities and into the fire. Paul embraced this idea because he knew that only by suffering could he share intimately in the experiences of Christ, who suffered on our behalf. He was so in love with the Savior that he longed to know the height and depth of Christ's own experience. Christ himself had "learned obedience from what he suffered" (Heb. 5:8). How we, too, can learn!

To return to the Lewis quotation at the beginning of this chapter, if we don't know what is most important to us, we must find out! Implicit in this idea is that if Christ is not at the top, we must reprioritize or else the "second things" (relationships, jobs, etc.) will not be healthy and mutually encouraging.

Seeking a husband to meet all our needs will leave us sorely disappointed. Instead, cling to Christ—in singleness and marriage. Remember, we are not promised a husband if we put God first. Love God and leave the second things to him.

Meditation Moments

1. In light of this chapter's focus on time with the Lord, read Psalm 119:24 as a starting place. What does this verse mean for your life? How can the Word counsel you? If accepting God's Word seems to be a burden for you, what might be the implications of this verse?

2. If you have not already done so, write out all instances of the Lord's past faithfulness to you. He will continue to be faithful!

3. What areas are weakest for you as you pursue your relationship with God: time with him, Scripture study, praying, praying the Word, Scripture memory, or seeking community? What steps will you take to further enrich these areas of your spiritual life?

7 The Joy Set before Us

●●●●●●●●●●●●●●●

My Heritage Forever

Brainstorm for a minute a few of your desires—not for material possessions, but for intangibles or character traits. Take out a piece of paper and begin a list, using these guidelines:

1. Think about what you desire before the Lord, and list these desires.
2. If you were to read your own epitaph, what qualities would you hope were acknowledged? List these qualities separately.
3. Compare the lists, refining and then combining them.
4. Prioritize the new list. Which desires are at the core? How would you truly like to be remembered?
5. What did you learn?

The list is to be between you and God. Take these desires to the Word of God to see what the Lord says of them. This can serve to strengthen your relationship with God and make you more aware of your heart.

Let's look at a Scripture passage to see how we can realize and cultivate the desires that line up with God's character. Here are a few desires from Psalm 19:

- A revived soul
- Wisdom
- A joyful heart
- Eyes that truly see

At the core of our being, all of us probably hope for at least some of these godly characteristics. According to this psalm, the way to find them is by following the Lord's law/statutes/precepts/commands, which are sure, altogether righteous, much more precious than pure gold, and sweeter than honey from the comb. Hand in hand is the fear of the Lord, which is pure and enduring forever.

Many people long for the joy and blessings that flow from a Christian heritage, but Scripture is described as the heritage available to all of us. "Your statutes are my heritage forever; they are the joy of my heart" (Ps. 119:111). The Word is a possession that we have received from the Lord from which we can draw provisions for life. Obedience to the Word is not "works righteousness" (earning our salvation by adherence to the law), but it does guide us in what is best and life-giving. Of course, we must remember that we cannot keep the Law perfectly; it is designed to ultimately point us to the perfect Law-keeper, Jesus. In addition, did you catch the three-letter word used to describe the emotion that God's statutes bring? *Joy!* Psalm 19:8 similarly displays this paradox: "The precepts of the LORD are right, giving joy to the heart." We so often think of the Law as a burden, but it is the very lens that shows us Christ, who offers us abundant life. In Proverbs 10:28 we read, "The prospect of the righteous is joy, but the hopes of the wicked come to nothing." True joy can be found *only* in Christ, no matter how it appears at present. At some point, the wicked will fall and realize the futility of their pursuits and dreams, which will lead to nothing.

The statutes of the Lord are trustworthy, not merely hollow regulations given by a harsh ruler. And he is trustworthy. He wants us to have life and have it to the full. "By [your Law] is your servant warned; in keeping [it] there is great reward" (Ps. 19:11). Why? Because following him brings life; his laws take my eyes off myself and direct them on to others and God. And in the end, these are the things that bring true joy.

After the admonishment to the disciples in John 15:10 that "if you obey my commands, you will remain in my love," Christ declares in verse 11, "I have told you this so that my *joy* may be in you and that your *joy* may be complete." That word again! Remember his display of ultimate obedience to the Father by enduring the cross for us, his joy? May we endure our own crosses in grateful, unbridled obedience for Christ, our joy!

> To him who is able to keep you from falling and to present you before his glorious presence without fault and with great *joy*—to the only God our Savior be glory, majesty, power and authority, through Jesus Christ our Lord, before all ages, now and forevermore! Amen. (Jude 24–25)

The Most Wonderful Time of the Year

Christmastime in New York City is special. Excitement is in the air; people are bustling about; all the stores and streets are filled with reminders of the season. During my first December of living in this city, I tried to soak up as much of the festivities as possible by attending Christmas parties, seeing the tree at Rockefeller Center, and going to Christmas shows, most notably the Radio City Music Hall Christmas Spectacular. As the show neared the end, I was amazed at the clear presentation of the first Christmas. It did *not* leave the Christ out of the Christmas story! Passages from Luke's gospel were read, shepherds came, wise men raised up their gifts before the Christ child, and even the live camels and sheep circled around the newborn baby King *in worship*! I was brought to tears.

This story is not only for those few lowly shepherds and foreign wise men. This good news is of *"great joy* that will be for *all the people"* (Luke 2:10). It has changed the course of history. The birth of this child has made its imprint on the whole world in each century since. "You have enlarged the nation and increased their joy. . . . For to us a child is born" (Isa. 9:3, 6). This child is the source of joy.

This story is also not only for Christmastime. The birth of Jesus into this world foreshadowed the death of this same One so that we might be born again. I love this observation by C. S. Lewis: "The Son of God became a man to enable men to become sons of God."[1] The birth of Christ means that *all* people might draw near to God in worship through Christ: despised and rejected shepherds—the lowest of Jewish society—foreigners who were once outside of the people of God, dignitaries, and we single women of the twenty-first century.

Do you realize what this means? Our lives can be changed *forever* because of the birth of Christ, which led also to his death and resurrection. This should usher joy unspeakable into our hearts and lives. Read the response of the shepherds: "The shepherds returned, glorifying and praising God for all the things they had heard and seen, which were just as they

1. C. S. Lewis, *Mere Christianity* (New York: Macmillan Publishing Company, 1952), 154.

had been told" (Luke 2:20). Through Scripture, we too have heard and seen what God has done and even now can observe his work in lives around us!

If you are unsure that God is at work and real, ask him to show you whether or not these things are true. Regardless of the time of year, read the story of Christ's birth again and meditate on its meaning for your life today. It is indeed news of *great joy*!

J.O.Y.

When I was in junior high school, our church group was called "J.O.Y." It simply stood for *Jesus*, *Others*, and then *You*. It was a good acronym reminder for ordering of priorities. And truly, if we were able to consistently keep the Lord first and then others, we would live abundant, servant lives. This is a lasting source of joy for our lives on this earth. Instead, we become so wrapped up in our own agendas and concerns that we forget those who will last for eternity. Catherine Marshall wrote:

> I have observed that when any of us embarks on the pursuit of happiness for ourselves, it eludes us. Often I've asked myself why. It must be because happiness comes to us only as a dividend. When we become absorbed in something demanding and worthwhile above and beyond ourselves, happiness seems to be there as a by-product of the self-giving.[2]

From Paul in his letter to the Thessalonians, we learn that those believers were his joy. "For what is our hope, our joy, or the crown in which we will glory in the presence of our Lord Jesus when he comes? Is it not you? Indeed, you are our glory

2. Catherine Marshall, "Happiness Is . . . ," in *Women's Devotional Bible* (Grand Rapids: Chosen Books, 1994), 1048.

and joy" (1 Thess. 2:19-20). Oh, that we would delight in others as much! Have we ever invested enough in Christ and others to have this passion and overflowing love for them? I fear that we are still looking into our own circumstances hoping for joy—but that will not last.

Consider Christ:

> who for the joy set before him endured the cross, scorning its shame, and sat down at the right hand of the throne of God. Consider him who endured such opposition from sinful men, so that you will not grow weary and lose heart. (Heb. 12:2b-3)

To what does "the joy set before him" refer? Our Lord lacked only one possession before his journey to this world; he was set to gain only one prize through giving up all he possessed: *us*! We were the reason that he continued to the cross. We were for him *joy*! This should make our hearts over-*joy*ed! I truly believe that we, too, have joy set before us—life everlasting with Christ that makes our journey worth it. We are coming closer to him, and he draws us closer even here on this earth.

Journey with Joy

Even though joy is set before us and abundant joy is available for us now, we are still on a journey—a race, as the author calls it in Hebrews 12:1-2a:

> Therefore, since we are surrounded by such a great cloud of witnesses, let us throw off everything that hinders and the sin that so easily entangles, and let us run with perseverance the race marked out for us. Let us fix our eyes on Jesus, the author and perfecter of our faith.

For the race, we must:

Throw off what hinders. This includes worry, anxiety, self-reliance, comparison, and discouragement because life is not as we had planned. A possible hindrance in running the Lord's race is looking for the approval of others. "If I were still trying to please men, I would not be a servant of Christ" (Gal. 1:10b). Another hindrance could be absorption with finding a husband to the detriment of serving the Lord.

Throw off the sin that so easily entangles. Judgment, gossip, bitterness, and greed are sins that have discontentment at their root. Refer back to chapter 3 for a review on sin if needed. It is like a sticky spider's web that wraps around us, making us immobile and ineffective. It is not likely that one so trapped will be able to run the race with joy.

Run with perseverance. It is a daily race that requires determination and willingness to pick up your feet and go, regardless of the circumstances. Be encouraged from this passage to get on your feet and be a part of this great race! Don't let it pass you by; don't hope that you will be swept away with it. It requires sweat, sometimes even injuries. But the Lord himself will bind up our wounds (Ps. 147:3) and "wipe every tear" from our eyes (Rev. 21:4).

Notice that sin *easily* entangles, in contrast to the race that demands perseverance. Sin is an easy trap; the race is hard. The comfort is that the race is already marked out. We are not going into a dark forest without a road map. First, Christ has gone before; he authored and is perfecting your faith. You have God's Word as a guide, as well as the Holy Spirit. Additionally, a great cloud of witnesses surrounds us to encourage us along the way. Jump into the race! It is an exciting one with Christ at the finish line. Yes, it is hard, but imagine Moses, Esther, and Jesus (to name a few) in the stands cheering you on.

And we are not running the race alone; others around us are running with us, not only those who have gone before. Several of my friends are involved in triathlons, marathons, and even Iron Mans, much to my awe! Each of them knows the importance of training with others instead of going it alone. They have experienced the bonding that results from the intense hours together working toward a goal. Let us join together in the training and race toward heaven.

Racing requires seasons of training and preparation, as well as endurance during the actual race. So, too, with our spiritual lives. There are different seasons; sometimes we will have a burst of energy; sometimes the weather will be rough. But we *must* keep our eyes *fixed* on Christ. He has run the race ahead of us, his *joy*! The more intense the suffering and tears, the sweeter the victory at the end. "The possibility of [sorrow and failure] is necessary to the joy of deliverance."[3]

Reaping with Songs of Joy

You may be going through an intensely difficult season when joy seems utterly out of reach and impossible. I encourage you to continue to seek the Lord, for I truly believe and have seen evidence in my own life that there is joy to be found on this earth. It is a joy in the Lord, not primarily in life's circumstances; it is a joy that looks beyond this life to the one to come. But the benefits can be realized now. "Come, let us sing for joy to the LORD." Why? "For the LORD is the great God, the great King above all gods" (Ps. 95:1, 3).

In my twenties, I had many long days of sadness, wondering about the purpose of my life. Many tears were shed and

3. J. R. R. Tolkien, *The Tolkien Reader* (New York: Random House, 1966), 86.

prayers of anguish lifted before the Lord. I can honestly say as I look back that the Lord heard my prayers; he was not silent. Even though the season lasted for several years, it was just a season—one of testing and refining. At times such as these, often we can only pray believing God is hearing because he has said so. It may not feel or appear as though he hears. But believe!

What does Scripture promise? "Those who sow in tears will reap with songs of joy. He who goes out weeping, carrying seed to sow, will return with songs of joy, carrying sheaves with him" (Ps. 126:5-6). I cannot promise when this will come to pass, but it will! Don't look for your circumstances to alter, but for your sight to change. Set your eyes on the Lord! Seek joy in him and his Word! After years of sowing in tears, I returned from the desert with songs of joy. Yet this is not to say that I will never again experience a long trial when the Lord will need to refine me by that method or use me in the midst of a desert.

God's Word will bring joy—even in times of great distress. "When anxiety was great within me, your consolation brought joy to my soul" (Ps. 94:19). The Lord consoles us through his Word. James in his letter encourages us to "consider it pure joy, my brothers, whenever you face trials of many kinds, because you know that the testing of your faith develops perseverance" (James 1:2-3). The joy will flow in or from these trials only when we realize the goodness of God to perfect us—and when we desire to be sanctified or conformed more fully to the image of Christ.

> Though you have not seen him, you love him; and even though you do not see him now, you believe in him and are filled with an inexpressible and glorious joy, for you are receiving the goal of your faith, the salvation of your souls. (1 Peter 1:8-9)

Did you notice the present-tense reality that we are *now* receiving the salvation of our souls? God is at work, perfecting every part of us.

Believe it or not, Scripture actually says that joy can be found in the circumstances of this life. Solomon wrote:

> So I commend the enjoyment of life, because nothing is better for a man under the sun than to eat and drink and be glad. Then joy will accompany him in his work all the days of the life God has given him under the sun. (Eccl. 8:15)

God has given us blessings here on this earth to be enjoyed: friendships, good food, the reality of living in the Lord, to name a few. *Don't* take these for granted! We become so absorbed in our personal frustrations that we forget or ignore the blessings right before our eyes. Recognize the call to be glad—to find the true reasons for gladness, and also to realize that *God* has given you these days on this earth. How will you use them for him?

Meditation Moments

1. Are you having a hard time feeling joyful or seeing joy in life? Why?
2. In what areas of your life have you been looking for joy?
3. Does your perspective on joy and life need to change? How can you pursue or embrace this change?
4. What blessings has God given you for which you can be thankful and joyful?

8 Footloose and Fancy-Free

● ● ● ● ● ● ● ● ● ● ● ● ● ● ●

In the World

I find the phrase "footloose and fancy-free" so appealing! I imagine a fun-loving woman with a sparkle in her eye and spring in her step, hitting the pavement without a care in the world. Doesn't that sound enticing? Maybe you think it's a far cry from your own life. But I do think many of us are much closer to being footloose and fancy-free than our attitudes or introspective lives reflect. Quite simply, for those of us who do not have children or parents for whom we must care, we have no dependents. Our time can be largely used at our discretion. We can live very selfish, independent lives without a care for another individual and with no one clamoring for our attention.

Instead, I want us to contemplate how we can use this time for the Lord and his kingdom. Do you realize that this "freedom" is an incredible gift? Let us live extravagantly for God! If you do marry someday, you will never again have such a time as this. So hit the pavement with many cares *for the world*!

Those Closest to Home

God has placed each of us in families. He did not do this randomly, regardless of your relationship with your family or its stability.

Most of us have skeletons in the family closet. An alcoholic distant relative may be lurking in the shadows, or it might hit home more directly: childhood pain suffered at the hand of a parent. Scars can run very deep, and healing is sometimes slow to come. But I encourage you to confront the past. It is extremely painful, but the benefits are innumerable. I recommend the study book *Breaking Free*,[1] by Beth Moore, as an excellent resource.

The truth is that God has called us to families. The single time of life can be a perfect time to wade through past pain—before we have our own families, Lord willing. I also mention this because I feel strongly that God would have us serve our families. They are the most logical place for our priority of service. Think creatively how you can be a blessing to a parent, grandparent, sibling, niece, or nephew. You could send a card—a rare occurrence these days with the ease and onslaught of e-mails. If you live in the same town, you could invite the family over for dinner, dessert, or a game night. You should definitely be calling your family members to stay in touch; let them know how you are doing; inquire and truly care about their lives. Do not put off until tomorrow what you can do today, for tomorrow might be too late.

Sisters in Christ

Be devoted to one another in [sisterly] love. Honor one another above yourselves. (Rom. 12:10)

1. Beth Moore, *Breaking Free* (Nashville: LifeWay, 1999).

How do we work out the implications of this verse in our lives? *Devoted* means "zealous or ardent in attachment."[2] Devotion is not lighthearted but fully intentional and passionate. Our example, of course, is Christ, who gave up all glory and perfect union with God for us—in order to be beaten and bruised and crucified for his own.

We will probably not be beaten for reaching out to others, but doing so is not always rewarding and can be very challenging. Being in relationships is definitely time-consuming, but it is also life-giving. Recently I was discussing with some musicians that the deepest music-making is hard to achieve apart from relationship. The greatest level of musical passion and truth to the composer's intent can be reached much more effectively through collaboration at a heart level—through sharing and experiencing together. It is the same in team sports when all players must play for the benefit of the whole. Without this element, the full potential of the team's ability cannot be gained.

Jesus could have come into this world and lectured to the disciples in the temple. Instead, he spent three years in deep community with them. Christ understood the importance of relationships and invested his life in them—literally. Philippians 2:5-8 highlights the Lord's attitude regarding those he came to befriend and save. In light of your friendships with other women, meditate on those verses as well as the following:

> If you have any encouragement from being united with Christ, if any comfort from his love, if any fellowship with the Spirit, if any tenderness and compassion, then make my joy complete by being like-minded, having the same love, being one in spirit and purpose. Do nothing out of selfish ambition or vain conceit, but in humility consider others better than yourselves.

2. *The Random House Dictionary* (New York: Ballantine Books, 1980), 241.

Each of you should look not only to your own interests, but also to the interests of others. (Phil. 2:1–4)

This is not a quest to see how many friends you can accumulate, how many people call you, or how many party invitations you receive. We are called to serve one another, to seek the interests of others above ourselves. This is sacrificial love. What are your friends' interests? If they love to spend time near the water, figure out a time for a day trip to a body of water. If they have had a difficult breakup, pray for or with them; phone them occasionally to check in. Think creatively about how you can go out of your way to consider your girl-friends better than yourself and to honor them.

I have found that very few people actually take the initiative in friendships. Do something novel: be the one to call up a girlfriend or arrange a special evening out with the gals! If you are lonely, don't wait for someone to call you; that is such an old, tiresome game. A fabulous idea for Valentine's Day is to plan a special meal for your single girlfriends. Pick a nice menu that is within your price range, buy a flower for each one, and have a place card for each with a special, personalized note. Why should you all sit at home alone on this day made popular by marketing and advertising? Another idea is to write your friends encouraging notes or letters. Remember birthdays. Call up a friend to go on a walk. Offer to help someone go shopping for a specific item she needs. In short, think of your friends and creatively plan time together and ways to encourage them. God has given us each other to walk along this road of life. Don't go it alone.

Church Ministries

An ideal setting for sacrificial love and service is in the church. We should throw away the mentality that church is only for worship on Sundays. The church is the whole body of believers consisting of many local bodies across the entire planet. If you are not in a church, find one *now* that holds to the Scripture as the inerrant Word of God. God intended for us to be encouraged and upheld by the church. It is vital for our spiritual health, for there we receive teaching, admonishment, and interaction with other believers. I strongly urge you *not* to be a church consumer, attending sporadically, only whenever your favorite preacher is in the pulpit, or switching churches at the drop of a hat—when, for example, they stop singing your favorite song.

The idea of commitment to any person or institution has become seriously cheapened. We do not feel the need to invest in people for the long haul (for example, through Bible study or accountability groups). Fewer and fewer churchgoers see the importance of committing to a church body. We have become consumers in every facet of life: "What can I get out of it?"—rather than "How can I give of myself?" If we don't like the preacher, the music, or the people, we move on to the next church. This is a tragedy.

We are consumed with self-gratification and have ceased to care about serving. Worshiping God, growing in him, and building community must be the motivations for our church attendance. As admonished in the Philippians passage above, we are called to serve one another, and this includes the church body. There are numerous needs within the church. Allow me to name alphabetically just a few:

- Adult choir
- Bereavement ministry
- Children's choir
- Elderly visitation
- Graphic design
- Hospitality/greeting team

- Hospital visitation
- Meals ministry
- Media ministry
- Mercy and justice
- Missions team
- Music ministry
- Nursery/children's ministry
- Office assistance
- Setup/teardown crews
- Special events planning
- Summer Bible school
- Tutoring
- Women's ministry
- Youth group

If one of these ministries sounds interesting to you, but your church does not currently offer it, request to start it up! Ask the Lord where he is calling you; there is a place of service in the church for all of us. Let us open our lives up to one another. Christ has called us to a rather radical type of community that is different from what the world provides; we are to be a city on a hill (Matt. 5:14)—set apart and deeply woven into each other's lives. We are to "rejoice with those who rejoice [and] mourn with those who mourn" (Rom. 12:15). Do not be content to associate merely on a social level; involve yourself in the dailyness and heartaches of others' lives.

Mercy and Justice

He has showed you, O man, what is good.
    And what does the LORD require of you?
To act justly and to love mercy
    and to walk humbly with your God. (Mic. 6:8)

116

Three things are required: to act justly, love mercy, and walk humbly with God. So concise, yet so hard. Why? Because we don't realize the *justice* that we deserve: condemnation. Abundant *mercy* instead has been shown: "While we were still sinners [despised and rejected], Christ died for us" (Rom. 5:8). Our inability to accept these truths makes us unwilling to *walk humbly* with God in realization of and gratitude for all he has done. The Christian life is about realizing the truth of our status before God and then allowing that truth to affect every other facet. If we grasped only a part of the incredible depth of his love, our lives would be a continual outpouring of service to others.

In so many ways, the church has failed in its calling to help the poor. I am among the most guilty and am ashamed to admit how the Lord specifically brought this sin to light in my own life recently. As I walked the streets of New York, familiarizing myself with the city, I noticed that I usually scanned the crowds for attractive men who might notice me. To what healthy, uplifting, and godly end were these efforts? My longing for someone to notice me will perish. I will be answerable to God on judgment day for the time I have wasted on frivolous pursuits. But for the grace and blood of Christ, I could not stand. It is true that we will not be condemned to hell for these sins if we are the Lord's children, *but* we miss innumerable blessings in this life by obsessing with ourselves! I could have spent the hours praying for the needy people I encountered, instead of looking past them for only those desirable in my eyes.

Whom does Jesus see? The helpless, unlovely, and dying. Oh, that we would have his heart and daily give him our calloused, self-absorbed selves. Much of our struggle with singleness may well have to do with our constant introspection; we spend much of our time pitying ourselves. God loves the outcast, the poor, the widowed, the needy. So should we. In fact, *we* are the needy, apart from God. "I know that the LORD secures justice for the poor and upholds the cause of the needy" (Ps. 140:12).

It seems so much easier to sit at home and write a check to the food bank or homeless shelter, but Christ went to the poor in person; he came to this earth, in fact, as a poor man. "He had no beauty or majesty to attract us to him, nothing in his appearance that we should desire him" (Isa. 53:2b). And yet we remain in our pristine existences. I'm afraid I would have kept my distance from the Lord had I lived during his days on earth, especially when he healed the sick and lame or said a kind word to a homeless person. And yet he came to me in my filth and lifted me out of the pit of my sinful life. He came for the poor and weak of the world. His is an upside-down kingdom, where the lowly are given seats of honor.

We must ask the Lord to give us open eyes to see the hurting and to give us willing hands to reach out to them. Commit to pray for individuals whom you initially scorn inwardly; this is at least a start. Then seek a ministry with which you can be involved. Ask your friends or Bible study to join you. If your church does not have a mercy ministry, ask the pastor whether it has been considered. Christ's whole ministry is one of mercy—to sinners and outcasts, which we all have been.

Let us be freed to go out and serve the unlovely, the untouchable. Christ today would visit an AIDS victim or eat with a prostitute in the inner city. He would love the wheelchair-bound one-eyed man I saw on Fifth Avenue, or even the drugged-up person I saw on the subway whose stench filled the whole car. These are graphic examples, but these two individuals represent the kind of needy people whom we all have encountered. What is our response?

The Mission Field

"The harvest is plentiful but the workers are few." (Matt. 9:37)

If you do not know any missionaries, do some research. We should all be at the very least aware of the work of bringing in the harvest worldwide. It is very encouraging to hear stories from around the globe.

Take the opportunity, if available, to see firsthand. Missions trips can offer wonderful opportunities for service and also tremendous personal spiritual growth. They can broaden your view of the world and the workings of the Lord in his world. I recommend that all of us consider going on at least one missions trip. Stretch your horizons and see what God is up to in other places.

Again, if your church does not have any mission trips, try to organize one through a mission organization. Otherwise, seek out trips through another church or agency.

In the Workplace

You do not have to be a full-time missionary to be on the mission field. We are servants and ministers of the gospel wherever we are. For those of us who are currently employed, God has placed us in a specific job. Some of you work in corporate America; others hold positions in not-for-profit agencies; many are in service jobs, such as health care. Whatever your position and environment, your job has significance before the Lord and has an impact in this world. We need store clerks, teachers, trash collectors, artists, and nurses, as well as every other profession that positively influences and provides for the world.

We may be dissatisfied with our jobs. Believe me, I have been there! But God has you at your workplace for the time being. This does not mean that you cannot be searching for a place where God could better use your gifts and abilities or a position in which you can personally gain more satisfaction. Pray, however, that the Lord would give you gratitude for the provision you have. Many people are without employment. If you are such a person, may the Lord bless you abundantly with work. Pray fervently and trust him for his provision.

I encourage all of us to ask the Lord to show us our gifts and how they may be utilized in the work environment. Although you must be prudent and pay the bills, don't seek a position based solely on the salary. Is it truly a job in which you will be able to best glorify God? Jesus told a parable in Matthew 25:14-30 of a master who entrusted his property to his servants. One "put his money to work and gained five more. So also, the one with the two talents gained two more. But the man who had received the one talent went off, dug a hole in the ground and hid his master's money" (vv. 16–18). What skills, money, or talents has the Lord given to you, and how will you use them for his glory? Seek to multiply these gifts in a job that fits and makes sense with your gifting.

We have unique opportunities to be salt and light in the work environment. God surrounds us at work with individuals who need to be loved. It is very easy to be comfortable with our church friends and compartmentalize our lives into church and nonchurch activities. Work is relegated to merely the place where I spend much of my week in order to make money or climb the corporate ladder. But God is not in the business of compartmentalization! He seeks to permeate the whole of our lives—every area and corner. Allow him to enter your workplace and transform your relationships, dealings, speech, and work ethic. We are called to be lights and the aroma of Christ in this world; few places are better suited to this calling than our workplaces.

You can make a conscientious effort to build friendships with coworkers by going to lunch occasionally, for example, or even by spending time together socially outside of work. Ask God to allow you to have spiritual conversations; he will rarely deny you this opportunity! Take time to stop by someone's desk and truly ask how the person is. In a past job, I found that I was so bound by my "to do" list that I had few friendships after four years of employment. This is, frankly, deplorable.

Also find ways to bring your coworkers into situations with your Christian friends. You can begin by arranging a social event, such as hosting a party in your home or sending an invitation to meet in the park for a picnic. The community that we experience and often take for granted can be a breath of fresh air to someone whose usual social venue is the bar scene.

Pursuing Your Passions

I do believe that God wants us to enjoy his world and live fully and freely. This does involve pursuing our passions. Unfortunately, we cannot all be in a profession that fits like a glove with all our gifts. Therefore, make sure you are pursuing activities and ministries outside of work about which you are passionate. I myself love to sing, so I determined a few years ago to be involved in opera on at least a volunteer basis. As it turns out, I am now pursuing a career in this field. Until that happens, *if* it ever happens, I have another job that I can do well and one in which I can serve effectively. My father has become involved in nature conservancy and spends hours leading hikes, helping with Eagle Days for kids, and clearing the park trails. This correlates with God's call for us to care for his earth. How can the activities you enjoy work in tandem with God's plan or give you a larger view of the world?

121

Think over your life and all the opportunities that God has given you, the passions he has placed in your heart, the activities you enjoy, the ways you like to serve people, the times you have been most fulfilled. God has given all of us ways in which we can explore his creativity and beauty in this world. Discover how he has shaped you. Begin an adventure of uncovering your interests. You may enjoy entertaining, love to cook, and have the gift of hospitality. Do not wait until you are married, but welcome people into your home *now*. Hospitality and food prepared as a work of art can nourish the soul. If you enjoy outdoor activities, spend time in nature enjoying all the variety that the Lord has created. Praise him for his beauty and think about encouraging others, too, by starting an outdoors club. Do you like to travel? See if you can plan vacations (within reason and your pocketbook) to discover the world that God has knit together and all the cultures represented. Perhaps you are gifted in sewing-type projects. Knitting has recently found its resurgence, so join a knitting club or make a blanket for a loved one.

Take the time to pull out some paper or a journal and truly meditate on these things, writing down your thoughts. This exercise can help you determine how to spend your time—in fact, how you should spend your life. God has given each of us unique gifts to be used for his kingdom. Don't waste any more time. *Carpe Diem*: seize the day. Live life to the fullest for the Lord and the benefit of others. Find the delight in life; there is such an abundance! God has made beauty and each one beautiful. Seek out beauty, *create it*, and share it with others.

Meditation Moments

1. How is God calling you right now to use this time on the earth that he has given you?

2. Do you need to make any changes? What is holding you back?

3. What are your passions?

4. In what ways can you serve:
   - Your family?
   - Your sisters in Christ?
   - At your church?
   - In your work?
   - Through your hobbies?

9 New Attitude

PHYLLIS GOLDEN, a dear woman I met at a church I formerly attended, wrote in a letter the following, which seems to beautifully summarize much of this book:

> Sometimes life is very hard to understand and I don't believe we are meant to understand all of it or there would be no call for faith. . . . [But] seize every moment you have and use every gift you have to love God and love your family, neighbors and friends while you can. There is no guarantee of tomorrow. Yet it is so easy to let the little, urgent, yet petty details of our lives take over. We are lulled into a false sense of security that everyone and everything will be there tomorrow. . . .
>
> Once I heard it said that life is what happens while we're making other plans. Please don't let the really important people, priorities, and relationships wait in your life. Enjoy every beautiful moment that God blesses you with and praise him for it.

To this I say: *Amen!* Let us grab hold of the promises of God and hold his hand firmly. *He will not fail us!*

At the Proper Time

Recently I was unemployed and searching for a job. Countless e-mails and contacts had been made to various banks, arts organizations, friends of friends, and so on. But—nothing. I received few returned calls or e-mails. Then, out of the blue, someone called me regarding a position about which I knew nothing in an area I had not considered. Within a day, I had applied, interviewed, and received an offer! Isn't it marvelous when God intervenes in that way? Sometimes the doors open more slowly and the final outcome doesn't seem so obvious at the beginning or along the path. But I truly believe, and have seen in my own life, that God will direct our lives down his course in the proper time and that we will see this direction unfold as we live before him, attempting to seek him with all our hearts. "We cannot tamper with God's clock. We have to be content to wait for his time. And meanwhile we are to pursue all the more conscientiously our duties on earth."[1] God does all things well in his time—and the timing is proper and perfect.

The Lord's proper timing is clearly presented in Luke 1:

Verse 5: "In the *time* of Herod king of Judea"—not during the reign of King Solomon or during the time of Queen Esther, but during the time of Herod, God brought the promised prophet into the world to prepare the way for the coming of Christ.

Verses 8–11: When Zechariah's priestly division was up for service, "*then* an angel of the Lord appeared to him," not when he was at home or when he was walking along to the marketplace, but while he was serving in the temple. No one else was privy to this encounter, since Zechariah was in the inner court, but all would know of its occurrence

---

1. John Stott, *Life in Christ* (Eastbourne, UK: Kingsway, 1991), 63.

later when he returned to the assembled worshipers—as a mute man.

Verse 13: "Your prayer has been heard." This prayer had undoubtedly been lifted before God for years. Zechariah and Elizabeth were elderly, well past the age of childbearing. But *this* was God's timing. He had heard their prayer, and *now* he was answering in this way. Isn't it remarkable how much more profound this birth is *because* of God's timing?

Verse 20: This verse sums up the miracle of John's birth, the incarnation, and, in fact, all of history. It proclaims the perfection of God's plan and words, "which will come true at their proper *time.*"

Verse 23: God's timing came into play once more before the actual conception: "When his *time* of service was completed, he returned home." Even these details were under the Lord's purview. "*After this* his wife Elizabeth became pregnant" (v. 24).

Verses 26-27: "*In the sixth month*, God sent the angel Gabriel to Nazareth, a town in Galilee, to a virgin pledged to be married to a man named Joseph, a descendant of David." The story of redemption planned by God before the beginning of time was being unfolded—in the proper time!

Verse 57: "When it was *time* for Elizabeth to have her baby [not a minute sooner or later], she gave birth to a son." Miraculous, proper, and redemptive!

The circumstances of your life are not random happenings. God has a proper time for each event that occurs. Regarding singleness or marriage, he knows exactly the proper length of time for both. If we remember his goodness and passionate love for us, this knowledge will be a balm to our souls.

I would like to share the following excerpt from a timeless classic starring an enduring and beloved character. Maybe you have at times felt like Jean Valjean, lead character in *Les Misérables*:

> Jean Valjean had come to a pit. . . . It was a hole of mud in a cavern of night.
>
> Valjean felt the surface slip away from under him, water on top, sludge beneath. He had to go on. . . .
>
> The water reached his armpits and he felt himself sinking; it was all he could do to move. His own sturdiness that kept him upright was also an obstacle. Still carrying Marius, and by the use of unbelievable strength, he pressed on, sinking ever deeper. Only his head was now above water, and his two arms carrying Marius. . . .
>
> He went on, tilting his face upwards so that he could continue to breathe. . . . He made a last desperate effort, thrusting a foot forward, and it rested upon something solid—only just in time. He straightened and thrust with a kind of fury on this support, feeling that he had found the first step of a stairway back to life.
>
> In fact this foothold, reached at the supreme moment, was the other end of the floor. . . . Valjean was saved.
>
> Emerging from the water, he stumbled on a stone and fell on his knees. This he thought proper, and he stayed in this posture for some time, his spirit absorbed in the thought of God. Then he stood upright, shivering and foul, bowed beneath his burden, dripping with mire; but with his soul filled with a strange lightness.[2]

This is a beautiful illustration of our intense struggles in this life—and of the sovereign salvation of the Lord, at just the right time: time enough to save us, but also time to bring us to our knees before him at the end in thankfulness.

2. Victor Hugo, *Les Misérables* (London: Penguin Books, 1982), 1088–89.

We don't know the whole story yet. God may have you single expressly for the next step. Regarding my relatively late pursuit of opera training, if I had tried to walk down this path in my early twenties, neither my parents nor I would have been prepared mentally, emotionally, or spiritually. And I might have pigeonholed my potential, not even considering this style of singing. Had I been married, such a relocation and the circumstances of my present life would not have been possible, and I would have missed out on the abundant blessings that God has showered on me through this experience. I have formed amazing friendships, seen the Lord open numerous doors, had opportunities for urban ministry, and seen the inner workings of the city. I am unfettered and able to live fully and expectantly with spontaneity, watching as God unfolds my life. When you throw everything up to him, he will put all the pieces together and hand them back in remarkable ways.

Of course, as mentioned, there are seasons of disappointment and drought. In these times, try to remember to bring your questions before the Lord and seek his answers.

Do you care that I have no husband?
Yes, enough to be THE Husband.
Do you love me?
Yes, so much that I gave my Son for you.
Can I continue?
You cannot alone, but with me you can.
Will you ever show up?
I have shown up, I am, I will remain.
Have you forgotten me?
Not for a moment; but perhaps you have forgotten me.
Will I ever marry?
You are worried about many things, but only one thing is necessary: to sit at my feet.

129

The Waiting Room

The title of the article "The Waiting Room,"[3] by Glenn Hoburg, has stuck in my mind over the years. All of us have a definite picture of this place in our minds: sitting . . . and sitting . . . in a doctor's office, or waiting day after day in the visiting area of a hospital during a loved one's illness, or standing in line at the DMV for a driver's license. Every resident of a city with mass transit understands the inevitability of subway hassles and transportation snarls, requiring doses of extreme patience at times.

Assess your reactions to these or similar life circumstances. Are you one who immediately lays on the horn at the first sign of a traffic jam? Or does your blood boil if the line creeps down the aisle at the grocery store? We must think about how we respond. We can become angry, depressed, impatient, doubtful, or defeated. *Or* we can read a book we have brought along, strike up a conversation with a person in line, or use the extra time to pray for those around us. These may seem like petty situations, but they can lend us insight into our reactions toward the far more important waiting rooms in our lives from the Lord—those lasting months or years.

Waiting can sometimes be the precursor to a more bountiful view of God's goodness. I have long remembered a beautiful image that God gave me of the wonder that can come after waiting. When I was in high school, my family took a summer vacation to Washington, a state filled with innumerable examples of God's creativity and beauty. A few days into our trip, we started the drive from Seattle to Mount Rainier National Park. As we approached, the clouds seemed to increase, until they gathered together as a thick and ominous covering when we

3. Glenn Hoburg, "The Waiting Room," *Covenant Magazine* (August/ September 1997): 8.

entered the park. The mountain for which the park is named was nowhere to be seen! It was as if it had vanished. That in and of itself was remarkable: how could something supposedly so large be invisible? We were not too concerned, since we had three full days ahead of us in the park. After two days of no mountain, however, our disappointment was growing.

As we were eating dinner on the second evening, we noticed commotion outside. Our curiosity was piqued, so we joined the other tourists. Within seconds, the clouds had parted and there before us towered the glorious, stunning, snow-covered peak, standing twice as high as the surrounding mountain range. Its beauty was beyond description or imagination! Truly, the wait increased by leaps and bounds the glory of the moment and the view.

So, too, in our lives. God displays his majesty and beauty after periods of waiting. He withholds only to bless in the end. We will not know the length of the time of waiting; we are simply called to patience and belief. George Robertson, pastor of First Presbyterian Church in Augusta, Georgia, says that waiting tests our faith, loosens our grip on the world, and makes us thankful.

From Waiting to Creating

Although we do have waiting rooms in our lives, I do not think we are only to sit around as hermits, waiting for God to send a miracle. God may also be calling us to change those waiting rooms into productivity centers. You might be at a dead end vocationally, with no other opportunities presenting themselves. Begin thoughtfully and proactively searching out new possibilities or open up your mind to how you can serve— either creatively at work or in a ministry at church or in your community. Create opportunities for movement forward!

As a single woman, do *not* sit around waiting for your husband to come along. Do something productive. I spent much of my twenties "playing it safe," living in locations that seemed well-suited for finding a suitor. He did not come along, and, unfortunately, I wasted needless energy on worry and, ironically, waiting. Wouldn't we rather that our husbands find us pursuing the core of our being, the essence of our God-given personality and character, rather than existing in a state of complacency or practicality? I am not advocating irresponsible pursuit of our dreams, but we should seek out who God made us to be and the talents he has given us. Search out how those can line up with his kingdom work and your vocation. Interestingly, when we are where God would have us, these are one and the same, whether in corporate America or third-world missions work. Remember, our ministry field is anywhere God has placed us.

Use the wonderful gift of time that God has given you today—especially if you are in a "waiting room."

The Great Paradoxes of the Christian Life

So much of the Christian life is diametrically opposed to how we naturally think life should be. It is worthwhile to ponder a few of these points to help orient our minds toward God's thinking instead of that of the world. Let these be food for thought, and add a few others if you are so inclined:

- We want stability: a home, for example; God calls us to make our home in heaven. We are just passing through.
- We want a soul mate; God calls us to the body of Christ.
- We want to be comfortable financially, physically,

spiritually; God calls us to follow him. Christ's path was the way of the cross.

- We want to plan our lives and build our nest egg; God calls us to live by faith and give generously.

His is an upside-down kingdom, it has often been said. The bullet points above do not mean that you live carelessly, never seek marriage, or hope for instability, of course. And the desires mentioned are not wrong. But they should call you to question your motives for the ways you live. The question is always how I can live before the Lord with one foot in heaven and one still here on earth. Scripture is the great guidebook that the Lord has given us, but it does not contain formulas for every situation of life, so we must daily seek God regarding these and other life paradoxes.

Do Not Hold Back

One of the greatest paradoxes of the Bible is found in Isaiah 54:1:

> "Sing, O barren woman, you who never bore a child; burst into song, shout for joy, you who were never in labor; because more are the children of the desolate woman than of her who has a husband," says the LORD.

How can this be? In ancient times, a woman's standing and acceptance were determined almost solely by the number of her children. Those without offspring were disregarded and oppressed. In these verses, God declares that the barren woman has a special and exalted position, regardless of the custom of the day.

Even though this passage speaks specifically to the nation of Israel, God would not have declared this metaphor if it were not also true of our personal standing in his eyes. We, as barren, single women, are significant. In fact, I believe we can adopt the calling to Israel to enlarge our tents and stretch wide the curtains (v. 2, paraphrased), an encouragement to prepare for blessing, increased ministry, and a wider sphere of influence. "Do not hold back" (v. 2). This is great affirmation that bursting into song and shouting for joy (v. 1) is possible for the single woman! It is not a dream and an unrealistic goal; "do not hold back."

No longer do we need to be afraid of what people think of us or fear that we are a disgrace. "Do not be afraid; you will not suffer shame. Do not fear disgrace; you will not be humiliated. . . . For your Maker is your husband—the LORD Almighty is his name" (Isa. 54:4–5).

The Story of Our Lives

Our lives are completely safe and protected in God's hands. One of my dear friends wrote some precious thoughts for our Bible study group that I would like to share:

> It's curious to think that each of us is living a life that reads like no one else's on this planet. Some chapters are real page turners and require many pages to describe or relate only moments. In contrast, whole seasons in life may occupy only one paragraph on a page, but seem to occupy so much of our life in real-time. Do you know the seasons I mean? Through Jesus, the Lord is writing our books. It is a book he has loved, is loving, and will love to write . . . and we are each the protagonist![4]

"We are God's *workmanship*,[5] created in Christ Jesus to do good works, which God prepared in advance for us to do"

4. Molly Morkoski, e-mail message, January 3, 2005.
5. The Greek word for *workmanship* is *poema*, which means "beautiful poem" or "work of art." This is what we are to God!

(Eph. 2:10). God is "crafting us into works of art!"[6] This is very exciting! Regardless of your present circumstances, God has a plan and a purpose. My life verse, repeated countless times by my wonderful mother, is Jeremiah 29:11. Let the truth of these words from centuries past speak into your heart and into the story that God is writing in your life: "'For I know the plans I have for you,' declares the LORD, 'plans to prosper you and not to harm you, plans to give you hope and a future.'" Allow him to unfold his plan in your life, and participate in the journey with him.

Again, from the masterly tale of hobbits, when Frodo declares along the difficult road to the forsaken Mordor that he can't continue, his faithful friend Sam replies:

> It's like in the great stories, Mr. Frodo, the ones that really mattered. Full of darkness and danger they were. And sometimes you didn't even want to know the end, because how could the end be happy? How could the world go back to the way it was when so much bad happened? But in the end it is only a passing thing—this shadow. Even darkness must pass. A new day will come, and when the sun shines it will shine all the clearer.
>
> Folks in those stories had lots of chances of turning back, only they didn't. They kept going because they were holding on to something . . .—that there's some good in this world and it's worth fighting for.[7]

Rubbish

We each have hopes and dreams, things that we think are "worth fighting for." God uses passions in our lives to move us

6. Morkoski e-mail.
7. *The Lord of the Rings: The Two Towers*, directed by Peter Jackson (New Line Productions, 2002).

forward in his plan and use us for his kingdom. But too often we can lose sight of the higher plan, the purpose that God is working in his world. This happens when we hold too tightly to our own desires—those things that we think will make us happy—instead of remembering that each life is just one stroke in the masterwork of all of mankind painted across the canvas of the centuries. In 1 Samuel 1 and 2, Hannah, who endured scorn for her barrenness, laid aside her intense longing to raise a child and instead looked to God's kingdom work. She offered back to the Lord the child given to her, who later became one of the greatest prophets in Israel's history.

I am convinced that several reasons for wanting various possessions are selfish. Many people, for example, seek to profit from marriage: it might bring financial security or stability, the marital status will change how we are viewed (somehow, albeit falsely, elevating us in our own and others' eyes), and we hope to have children who will be beautiful and make us proud. I do not mean to downplay marriage, which is a good thing, but instead cut to the root of our reasons for marriage. Remember, it is instituted by God to be holy and for his purposes. One benefit is to bring us joy, yes, but this is *not* to be our sole desire. God intended for us to be helpers. Servanthood is completely selfless! He also seeks to increase his kingdom through children born into godly homes.

Do we want marriage to be merely for our own profit or at least for a little bit of personal gain?

> But whatever was to my profit I now consider loss for the sake of Christ. What is more, I consider everything a loss compared to the surpassing greatness of knowing Christ Jesus my Lord, for whose sake I have lost all things. I consider them rubbish, that I may gain Christ and be found in him, not having a righteousness of my own that comes from the law,

but that which is through faith in Christ—the righteousness that comes from God and is by faith. (Phil. 3:7–9)

Are we more enamored of the thought of knowing an earthly man rather than Christ Jesus our Lord? Paul states that it is surpassingly greater to know Christ. All other pursuits are regarded by him as *rubbish* in comparison. Again, this is not by any means to completely negate marriage, or any other good gift, but to cause us to analyze our priorities. Knowing God and loving him is far above *any* other earthly relationship, job, or ministry. Every other activity and relationship should flow out of our love for and pursuit of God.

Choose Life

For one year, most of my belongings were in an out-of-state storage unit, precipitated by a quick move and an unknown future location. At the end of a year, it became clear that the best course of action was to sell all the contents in the unit. As I anticipated this, I wrote the following in my journal:

> I am setting out this weekend to complete this arduous task. I have a choice before me today: to grumble and fret about closing a chapter of ten years with these things and this semblance of stability, and to worry about the future; or to rejoice in being freed of more ties to this world, hoping instead in my future glory, and waiting expectantly for what the Lord will bring into my life next.

What does the Lord speak to us?

> See, I set before you today life and prosperity, death and destruction. For I command you today to love the LORD your God, to walk in his ways, and to keep his commands, decrees and laws; then you will live and increase, and the

137

LORD your God will bless you in the land you are entering to possess. (Deut. 30:15–16)

The choice of grumbling in fact does lead to death and destruction—in our spirits and minds, and perhaps even in our actions. We become downtrodden and hopeless. This is *not* how God would have us live. We must choose a new perspective: to attempt to see the world and the events of our lives as vehicles for the Lord's presence with and work in us. The spiritual blessings will flow. "Now choose life, so . . . that you may love the LORD your God, listen to his voice, and hold fast to him. For the LORD is your life" (Deut. 30:19b–20). Do we believe that the Lord is indeed our life? Such a perspective will change the way we live.

Perspective

We bring certain opinions, stereotypes, and judgments to each and every situation before us. We have certain thoughts about food, other cultures or cities, even church denominations. For example, how often have you looked down on someone who does not share your style of worship? My stereotypes were greatly challenged while in college by interacting with some individuals from a very different spiritual background from my own. Thankfully, we were able to accept each other's differences and, in fact, became best of friends through our college years. I had to learn to see these women as made in the image of God and further, in this particular instance, as dear sisters in Christ.

It's important to ask whether these preconceived notions, driven by first impressions, are immovable to the end *or* whether we will open our minds and be willing to consider all angles and perspectives. Spiritually, we must be open to all God's devices and designs. What may seem like an obstruction can become a doorway. God's Spirit moves in different ways and at different times. This notion of perspective was made crystal clear to me by the epic presentation of "The Gates" by Christo and Jeanne-Claude, a display of seventy-five hundred "gates" stretching twenty-three miles in New York City's Central Park during February 2005. At first I was completely dissatisfied and appalled that anyone could find these steel impositions beautiful. One night at a Bible study, I made my definite opinion known and was shocked to hear one woman's response of complete adoration of this artwork. She even found it glorious and was moved to praise the Lord. Needless to say, I was moved to silence on the subject for the rest of the night.

But I was also determined to go back to "The Gates" with an open mind, willing this time to be affected—perhaps positively. I was astounded by what I learned—about myself and the world.

I realized that even if I did not find the structures beautiful at first or even generally, there were aspects of beauty. When the wind blew through the fabric, the drapery rustled in varying patterns and heights. Slowly, I found myself noticing the interesting effect made by the gates gradually tapering off and decreasing in visual size as they wound down the path beyond. Later, after a snowfall, I was awed at the contrast made by the saffron color against the glistening snow, painted behind by a brilliant blue sky. Then I found myself touched by the children, foreigners, New Yorkers, artists, rich, and poor—people of all types who had congregated in this one spot for this event.

The lesson I learned? We must be willing to come back to the gates in our lives several times, willing to be touched, changed, challenged, and shaped. I truly believe the Lord would have us look for the beauty and significance in everything, to open ourselves up to the bounty of life that he has put before us, to come alive and have a response! Interact with the circumstances, people, nature, and art around you. Always look to grow, even in your singleness. There is a wealth of opportunity and joy to embrace. Don't let life pass you by, and don't stand on the sidelines. Walk through the gates with open eyes to learn and absorb from those around you.

Don't Doubt the Thread

In George MacDonald's children's book *The Princess and the Goblin*, the little girl is told that she must follow her grandma's thread regardless of where it leads. She is taken down many winding paths, but remembers the exhortation "You must not doubt the thread."

Do you ever feel as though you are being led on a wild-goose chase? Perhaps you even feel like the wild goose at times—completely out of control or lost. Times like these require complete trust in the Lord's goodness, his timing, and the story he is writing in our lives. We can fight against him or go with him. I guarantee that the latter option is the way of joy and peace. It is not devoid of difficulty, but it is life lived to the full with our Savior.

I can honestly say that this time of singleness for me has been rich and abundant. But this is only because of the times of struggle and the glimpses God has given me of his work on my behalf. On the other side of every storm is a bright, shining sky that is glorious by comparison. Strangely, looking back, I find that the struggles don't seem as intense. Indelibly etched in my memory is a beautiful picture that God painted in his sky one foreboding summer evening when I felt lost in loneliness. The sky was thick with the darkest of rain clouds, but then a tiny opening appeared in the sea of clouds, light streamed in, and the glorious blue heavens were visible beyond.

God reminded me through his nature that he is beyond all suffering. There is life beyond the present—glorious, full, and free. The Lord himself holds the end of the thread.

This is the abundance that God wants for us. This is a unique time. Don't squelch the opportunities that God will bring your way.

Resolved

George Müller was a man of great faith who gave all he had to run orphanages and serve abandoned children. He said once, "There was a day when I died, *utterly died* . . . ; died to George Müller, his opinions, preferences, tastes and will—died to the world, its approval or censor—died to the approval or blame even of brethren or friends. . . ."[8] He modeled his life after Christ, who left all glory and power to become lowly for us. We can squander our time, talents, and treasures; we can live lives of worry and self-absorption; or we can love freely and look beyond ourselves, recognizing all that Christ has first done for us.

Jonathan Edwards included the following in his resolutions of 1723:

> Resolved, never to lose one moment of time; but improve it the most profitable way I possibly can;
> Resolved, to live with all my might, while I do live;
> Resolved, to endeavor to obtain for myself (as much happiness in the other world), as I possibly can, with all the power, might, vigor, vehemence, yea violence, I am capable of, or can bring myself to exert, in any way that can be thought of.[9]

8. Arthur Tappan Pierson, *George Müller of Bristol* (London: J. Nisbet & Co., 1899), 367.

9. John Piper and Justin Taylor, *A God-Entranced Vision of All Things: The Legacy of Jonathan Edwards* (Wheaton, IL: Crossway, 2004), 124.

So, then, live—passionately and energetically—as one whose soul is the Lord's. You have been bought with a price; you are no longer your own (1 Cor. 6:19–20). Discover how God has made you singly and uniquely *you* (Ps. 139:13–16)! He has given you this time, place, and season. How will you serve him *now*?

Meditation Moments

1. Recall a time in your life when you sensed the specific evidence of the Lord's ordained timing. Recall another time when you sensed that you were in a "waiting room." Did you walk through each of these seasons with a proper perspective and faith?
2. What paradoxes of the Christian life can be added to those mentioned on pages 132–33?
3. In which personal life instances can you "choose life" instead of responses such as discouragement, complaining, or frustration?
4. Think of daily, life, and relational situations in which you draw immediate conclusions instead of considering all angles. How can your perspective change your view of these circumstances?
5. What thought patterns that have impeded you from trusting God in your singleness are being challenged by him? What are some concrete ways you can resolve to live life to the fullest?